WEDGWOOD
A COLLECTOR'S GUIDE

WEDGWOOD
A COLLECTOR'S GUIDE

PETER WILLIAMS

A QUANTUM BOOK

Published by Shooting Star Press, Inc.
230 Fifth Avenue, Suite 1212
New York, NY 10001
USA

ISBN 1-57335-519-4

This book was produced by
Quantum Books Ltd
6 Blundell Street
London N7 9BH

Creative Director: Richard Dewing
Designer: Stuart Walden
Project Editor: William Hemsley
Editor: Patricia Bayer
Picture Researcher: Dee Robinson

Typeset in Great Britain by
Central Southern Typesetters, Eastbourne
Manufactured in Hong Kong by
Regent Publishing Services Limited
Printed in Singapore by
Star Standard Industries Private Ltd

This book was reprinted in 1996 due to popular demand.
The price guide at the back of the book was compiled at the time of
original publication in 1992 and should therefore be used only as a
rough guide to today's prices. If in doubt, please contact your local
dealer for a more accurate estimate.

CONTENTS

Introduction

The Wedgwood trade name has justly become synonymous with blue stoneware pottery decorated with classical white relief work in the manner perfected by Josiah Wedgwood I over two hundred years ago. While it is true that such "jasperware" continues to form a reasonably predictable portion of Wedgwood's output, it is important not to overlook the wide variety of other ceramic products made by this company. Wedgwood's time-honored proprietors, designers, technicians and potters have always displayed creative innovation while maintaining traditional ideals. The purpose of this book is to introduce the reader to the complete range of Wedgwood ware, both ornamental and useful, and also to the many personalities responsible for the design and manufacture of the pieces.

Newcomers to the collecting of ceramics will be surprised by the diversity they see in this book, and also intrigued by Wedgwood's artistic and entrepreneurial resourcefulness.

Those readers who were previously apprehensive about forming their own Wedgwood collection will find that they are not restricted to purely traditional lines. They will also gain confidence from the clearly presented information that covers all aspects of the firm's history, products, and techniques.

Large collections of Wedgwood ceramics have been formed by museums and private individuals worldwide. Some enthusiasts choose to concentrate on a particular period or theme; others, a particular type of material or technique. Existing devotees will find their interests rekindled by this book and may even decide to explore tangential aspects of their chosen subject.

Finally, those readers who simply enjoy using high quality functional ceramics in their homes can now learn about the evolution of the renowned Wedgwood tableware range – from the experimental cream-colored earthenware of the 1760s to the designer services of the 20th century.

1

Cane ware bough pot molded to simulate bamboo and painted with encaustic colors c1790 (RIGHT).

A Family of Staffordshire Potters

Portrait of Josiah Wedgwood I by Sir Joshua Reynolds, 1782.

Josiah Wedgwood I (1730–95)

I saw the field was spacious, and the soil so good, as to promise an ample recompense to anyone who should labour diligently in its cultivation.

(FROM THE EXPERIMENT BOOK OF JOSIAH WEDGWOOD I.)

The modern Wedgwood factory at Barlaston, six miles (1.6 km) south of Stoke-on-Trent in the northwest of England, is indebted to the talents and vision of Josiah Wedgwood I, the last of a dozen children born into the pot-making family of Thomas and Mary Stringer Wedgwood of the Churchyard works at Burslem, just north of Stoke. Josiah's schooling probably terminated in 1739 when, on the death of his father, he

---

WILLIAM GREATBATCH (1735–1813)

It is generally claimed that William Greatbatch was apprenticed to Thomas Whieldon and first met Josiah Wedgwood I at Fenton, but there is no documentary evidence to support this. Greatbatch may have been acting for Wedgwood in London as early as June 1760. It is certainly the case that in 1762 he began a close business association with Josiah I, as well as setting up a pottery in his own right at Lower Lane, Fenton. Greatbatch began to supply Wedgwood with a wide range of block molds and biscuit earthenware (for coloring and glazing at Burslem) and probably finished wares also. An arrangement between the two potters seems to have been maintained until the mid-1770s.

Greatbatch continued in business for 20 years but was declared bankrupt in 1782. By 1786 he had gained employment at Etruria, on very favorable terms, and probably became general manager from 1788 until his retirement in about 1807. Josiah I evidently had high regard for his colleague and allocated him a substantial pension.

2

Jasperware "Ruined Column" vase, a romantic example of neo-classicism, c1785.

entered the employment of his eldest brother, Thomas, who had inherited the family business. Josiah served an apprenticeship with Thomas, but formed a partnership with John Harrison and Thomas Alders of Cliffe Banke, Stoke, in 1752. Two years later he became partner to the master potter Thomas Whieldon at nearby Fenton.

During his five years with Whieldon a curious arrangement was made whereby Wedgwood could experiment with new ceramic bodies and glazes, to the benefit of both parties, but would not be obliged to reveal any secret formulae to Whieldon. It is likely that William Greatbatch, who later worked directly for Wedgwood, was serving his apprenticeship at Fenton at this time. "Wedgwood-Whieldon" products include white salt-glazed stoneware, agate ware, and "tortoise-shell" glazed cream-colored earthenware. Josiah eventually proved more enterprising than his partner and, prompted by disparaging public remarks directed toward the general potting standards of Staffordshire, returned to Burslem and set up on his own at the Ivy House works in 1759. These premises were rented from two fellow potters, his prosperous distant cousins, Thomas and John Wedgwood.

Initially, the Ivy House wares would have resembled those of Fenton, but with improved green and yellow glazes. However, by 1761 Josiah had introduced a superior inexpensive clear-glazed creamware body, containing pipeclay and ground flint, which soon succeeded delftware as the popular material for cheap ceramic tableware. Much of Wedgwood's creamware was sent to Liverpool for overglaze transfer printing by the firm of Sadler and Green. A vast quantity was printed for export to Continental Europe, Ireland, and America, and was therefore shipped directly from the port. Josiah's reputation for fine quality creamware had reached the Continent by at the latest 1764, as in that

A tray of Josiah Wedgwood I's jasperware trials. Years spent laboriously experimenting with the jasper body led Wedgwood to describe himself as "almost crazy" in 1774.

year a Dutch merchant enquired about ordering some transfer-printed, enameled and cauliflower-molded tea sets.

After gaining royal patronage from Queen Charlotte, Wedgwood was appointed "Potter to Her Majesty" in 1766 and, in turn, he named his creamware "Queen's ware." In 1773 he received his most challenging order for Queen's ware – the "Frog" Service, of nearly 1,000 pieces, for Catherine the Great, Empress of Russia.

In 1764, the year in which Josiah married his cousin Sarah, he transferred operations to the larger Brick House works in Burslem (later known as the "Bell" works because of the bell that was erected to summon its workmen). Alongside the production of Queen's ware, he continued disciplined scientific research with other ceramic bodies, especially black basaltes, which was first successfully produced in 1768. Wedgwood consciously divided his output into two distinct categories: "useful" ware and "ornamental" ware. The former continued in production at the Brick House works until the closure of the works in 1772. Manufacture of the latter was removed to the Etruria works, built on the 350-acre (142-hectare) Ridgehouse Estate situated between Burslem, Hanley, and Newcastle-under-Lyme, which Josiah had purchased five years earlier.

Portrait of Josiah Wedgwood I by George Stubbs enameled biscuit Queen's ware plaque, painted in the of 1780.

The Wedgwood and Bentley Partnership (1769–80)

If I had more time, more hands and more heads I could do something . . .

(JOSIAH WEDGWOOD I TO THOMAS BENTLEY ON THE DEVELOPMENT OF JASPERWARE, AUGUST 1774.)

Josiah Wedgwood did not enjoy good health. He contracted smallpox in childhood (possibly in the 1746–47 epidemic), leaving his

3

Two of the six encaustic-decorated black basaltes "First Day's Vases," thrown by Josiah Wedgwood I at the Etruria factory's inaugural ceremony on June 13, 1769.

right leg weak and troublesome, and incurred serious damage to his right knee in a riding accident during his time at Fenton. Throughout the resulting periods of enforced rest he read avidly, particularly about scientific progress. But physical confinement led to boredom and agitation, so in 1762 the surgeon Matthew Turner, who was attending Josiah in Liverpool, introduced him to Thomas Bentley, a learned local merchant and classicist.

Wedgwood and Bentley became firm friends, and the latter began to provide valuable export orders for Queen's ware. To encourage foreign trade, many designs were tailored to suit specific markets. At the same

Portrait of Thomas
Bentley attributed to
Joseph Wright of
Derby, 1778.

imitations of Greco-Roman cameos and
seals. But initial experiments met with only
limited success and nearly drove him to dis-
traction. However, satisfactory small flat
jasper pieces started to appear by 1775, and
Wedgwood soon gained full control over
production, utilizing the material for
ambitious ornamental pieces. Many of the
resulting shapes and subjects followed lines
that had already proved successful in other
bodies. His ultimate achievement in jasperware was the first edition of the still-famous
Portland Vase.

WILLIAM WOOD (1746–1829)

*Brother to Enoch Wood, a celebrated
Staffordshire potter and modeller, William
Wood was apprenticed to Josiah Wedgwood I
in Burslem and later became chief modeler of
useful wares. He also worked on the first
edition of the Portland Vase.*

---

time, America and Russia were found to be
useful outlets for styles that were no longer
fashionable in England. Bentley was urged
to accept orders for all kinds of pottery, as
any items that the Wedgwood factory could
not itself supply were simply purchased
from other Staffordshire potters.

Josiah's poor leg was eventually amputated
above the knee in 1768. When the Etruria
factory opened in 1769, Bentley personally
powered the potting wheel on which Josiah
threw six "First Day's Vases" at the inaugural
ceremony. After firing, these were sent to
London for painting at the Chelsea Decorating Studio. Bentley signed a formal partnership agreement with Wedgwood on August
10, 1769, concerning the manufacture of
ornamental pieces. After a brief spell in
Burslem, Bentley became Wedgwood's
London manager, overseeing the invaluable
retail and decorating establishments there
until his death in 1780.

Bentley remained in frequent commun-
ication with Josiah, encouraging a mutual
interest in classicism together with the development of Wedgwood's most renowned
product, jasperware. Ironically, he died prior
to its introduction as a material for fine neo-
classical vases. Wedgwood felt compelled to
master jasperware in order to compete in the
expanding marketplace for fashionable

The American
Revolution

*The Rattle Snake is in hand. I think it will be
best to keep such unchristian articles for Private
Trade (to sympathetic friends).*

*(JOSIAH WEDGWOOD TO THOMAS BENTLEY,
8 AUGUST 1777, REGARDING THE ISSUE OF JASPER
SEALS BEARING A COILED RATTLESNAKE AND
THE LEGEND "DON'T TREAD ON ME" – A
COMMON COLONIAL PROPAGANDA MOTIF.)*

The export of large quantities of utilitarian
English pottery to the American colonies
had begun long before Josiah Wedgwood
established his own fruitful market. By the
mid-1760s he and his neighbouring potters
were experiencing drastically reduced domestic sales and were therefore becoming re-
liant on their overseas orders. Thus, on hear-
ing reports that an English master potter was
trying to found a potworks in the New

4

Queen's ware teapot, over-glaze printed with the "Death of Wolfe" after Benjamin West, 1770s. Major-General James Wolfe was killed at the siege of Quebec in 1759.

5

Jasperware medallion of Benjamin Franklin, modeled by William Hackwood after Isaac Gosset, c1777. During the years of America's struggle for independence, Franklin traveled abroad to represent his country.

World, Josiah expressed his grave concern to Sir William Meredith in 1765. Such a works would lead to a devastating loss of trade, but the attempted project did not come to fruition and the export of Wedgwood "Crockery Ware" flourished. Indeed, by 1771 Queen's ware began to be advertised by name in the *New York Gazette*.

The closure of Boston harbor from 1774 to 1783 and the boycott of British goods during the War of Independence came as a great blow to Wedgwood. As a businessman, he had a vested interest in the re-establishment of peace; as a libertarian he sympathized with the rebellious colonists; as "Potter to Her Majesty" he remained a patriotic but skeptical Englishman. Ultimately, Josiah became exasperated by the attitude of the British politicians who, after the loss of millions of pounds and thousands of lives, proceeded to trivialize the whole event.

majority of these were purchased by British and French sympathizers.

The abolition of slavery was always close to Josiah's heart. He was one of the ardent founders of the Society for the Suppression of the Slave Trade and in 1787 he issued jasper emancipation badges, or "Slave" medallions, distributed to anybody concerned with the cause. A packet of these medallions was sent to Benjamin Franklin for his campaign against slavery in the United States.

Josiah Wedgwood II (1769–1843)

*Every day we are asked for China [porcelain])
Tea Ware – our sales of it would be immense if
we had any . . .*

(JOSIAH BYERLEY WRITING TO JOSIAH
WEDGWOOD II FROM LONDON IN 1811.)

With the closure of the Brick House works in 1772, the manufacture of both ornamental and utilitarian wares continued fully at Etruria. An extensive range of products was developed in various pottery bodies, including jasper-dip, cane ware, *rosso antico*, and pearl ware. In 1790 Josiah I took his three sons, John, Thomas, and Josiah II, into partnership together with his nephew Thomas Byerley, who had become London manager upon Thomas Bentley's death. John and Thomas Wedgwood both withdrew three years later, Thomas permanently in order to pursue primitive photographic experiments.

After his father's death in 1795, Josiah II moved to the south of England, leaving Thomas Byerley in control. However, without the assistance of his cousins, and at a time of European war and domestic social unrest, Byerley experienced foundering trade. John rejoined the firm in 1800 and did much to improve its failing fortunes. The adoption of underglaze transfer printing on pearl ware in 1805 helped Etruria to keep up with its competitors. In 1807 Byerley moved to Dublin to set up a showroom there. Josiah II returned home and later assumed sole responsibility at Etruria in 1812.

Josiah I had not chosen to undertake the manufacture of porcelain, although he was

THOMAS BYERLEY (1747–1810)

In 1768 Josiah I helped his nephew, Thomas Byerley, emigrate to America. Byerley was an aspiring writer and actor but he eventually settled in New York as a schoolmaster. He returned to England on the outbreak of the American War of Independence and was employed at Etruria before becoming the London manager on Thomas Bentley's death. Byerley was succeeded in London by his son, Josiah.

6

Jasperware Slave Emancipation Badge ("Slave Medallion") produced at Josiah Wedgwood I's own expense in 1787. The wearing of such medallions, mounted as jewelry, became very fashionable at that time. A number of similar black-on-white jasperware medallions were reproduced in 1959.

The cessation of hostilities and the resumption of normal business between the two countries after the Treaty of Paris and the 1783 Provisional Trade and Intercourse Bill came as a great relief to Josiah. He was soon exporting Queen's ware again, appropriately printed with heroic scenes such as "Washington in Glory and America in Tears." He also produced numerous black basaltes and jasper portrait medallions of revolutionaries such as Benjamin Franklin and Voltaire, but the

fully versed in its composition and application. Fine porcelain had previously satisfied rococo taste, but fell somewhat from favor with the onset of neo-classicism. Thus, Wedgwood pottery became the ceramic market leader, and Josiah I saw no good reason to diversify. In 1811 Thomas Byerley's son Josiah, who was then overseeing Wedgwood's London operation, reported that the capricious market was again demanding porcelain tableware. Josiah II realized the need for a new Wedgwood line and introduced bone china at Etruria in 1812. Limited production continued until into the 1820s, but the marketing was inadequate and the designs were too restrained for opulent Regency tastes. However, the manufacture of Wedgwood bone china was revived in 1878 and has continued successfully to the present day.

Francis Wedgwood (1800–88) and Sons

Painters ordinarily change their national character before the works of the Masters, their models . . . . Specially devoted to pottery, I have become English at Wedgwood's.

(EMILE LESSORE, FRENCH PAINTER, ACTIVE FOR WEDGWOOD, 1860–70.)

Josiah Wedgwood II took two of his sons, Josiah III and Francis, into partnership in 1823 and 1827, respectively. Josiah III showed little interest in the firm and withdrew shortly after his father's retirement in 1842, leaving his brother briefly in sole control. In 1843 Francis was partnered by John Boyle, formerly of the rival Stoke-on-Trent firm of Minton. Boyle died 18 months later and Wedgwood was joined by Robert Brown from 1846 to 1859. Francis took his eldest son, Godfrey, as a partner in 1859, and later his sons, Clement Francis and Lawrence.

View of the interior of the Wedgwood showroom on York Street, St James's Square, London, after the 1809 Ackermann print (TOP).

Josiah Wedgwood I and his family, by George Stubbs, oil on wood panels, painted in the autumn of 1780. Josiah and his wife, Sarah, are seated beneath the tree on the right (ABOVE).

EMILE AUBERT LESSORE (1805–76)

The French spirit of the Barbizon School of naturalistic painters was brought to the Potteries by artists such as Edouard Rischgitz (employed by Minton c1864–70) and Emile Lessore. The latter was born in Paris and studied under Hersent and Ingres. Lessore first painted on ceramics in Laurin's factory at Bourg-la-Reine, near Paris, and he later worked at Sèvres for six years from 1852. Following the death of his wife in 1858, he moved to England and was employed by Minton. However, he felt artistically constrained and oversupervised, so in the spring of 1860 he approached Wedgwood for work. His appointment was confirmed in August that year.

At Wedgwood, Lessore enjoyed artistic freedom, and he built up a decorative art studio that boosted the firm's national and international standing. A large selection of his work received widespread acclaim at the 1862 Paris Exhibition, and the retailer Phillips, of London, subsequently purchased the entire display. Lessore's only remaining complaint was the English climate, which had an adverse effect on his health, and he negotiated a flexible arrangement with Wedgwood that allowed him to return to Paris with the option of living in London in the summer.

In time, Lessore assumed a somewhat ambassadorial role and concentrated on providing outline sketches and designs suitable for enhancement by Wedgwood's work force. By 1867 demand for his style of work had declined, and two years later both parties reluctantly entered into a new agreement whereby he continued to work for Wedgwood in a very limited way only.

THOMAS ALLEN (1831–1915)

Regarded as the leading Staffordshire painter of the 19th century, Thomas Allen trained at the Stoke School of Art and won a National Art Training Scholarship in 1852. After studying at the South Kensington School of Design in London, he was employed by Minton as a figure painter. In 1876 he joined Wedgwood, and the firm thus gained a prestige replacement for Emile Lessore. He maintained his position as director of the Fine Art Studios (effectively art director) at Etruria for 20 years from 1878 and fully retired in 1904. Allen's figure work – often depicting romantic, scantily clad females – is predominant on vases and plaques, but he was also responsible for the development of tile and tableware designs at Etruria.

Before his retirement in 1870, Francis Wedgwood presided over some important introductions at Etruria, including Carrara ware, inlaid ware, Rockingham ware, and majolica ware. In 1860 he employed Emile Lessore, whose painterly works gained much prestige for Wedgwood at the various international exhibitions.

Godfrey, Clement Francis, and Lawrence were responsible for the reintroduction of bone china, the instigation of Victoria and Worcester-style ware, and the revival of tile production at Etruria. Clement Francis died in 1889, and two years later Godfrey withdrew, leaving Lawrence to form a partnership with his nephews, Cecil and Francis Hamilton Wedgwood. In 1895 the firm was incorporated as Josiah Wedgwood & Sons Ltd, and was afterward controlled by Cecil, Francis Hamilton, and Kennard Wedgwood (eldest son of Lawrence).

7

A monumental majolica "Swan" vase on pedestal, c1885. Standing 83½ in/ 2.12 m high, this is one of the largest pieces of majolica ware that Wedgwood ever produced (OPPOSITE).

8

Pair of Queen's ware vases, painted by Emile Lessore, c1875.

9

Two examples of Emile Lessore's genre painting on Wedgwood Queen's ware, c1870.

Wartime and Depression

They were leaders, they weren't pushers, they led from the front . . .
(TED LAWTON, MANAGER, DESCRIBING THE WEDGWOOD DIRECTORS.)

The consequences of two wars caused major setbacks to the company while the newly formed triumvirate was still in its infancy: first, export trade to the United States slumped as a direct result of the Spanish-American War; second, the management was severely weakened when Cecil and Francis Hamilton were called away to fight in the Boer War in southern Africa. They returned home to battle with their own busi-ness troubles and valiantly struggled to re-instate a successful Wedgwood market. In 1904 John Goodwin was employed to succeed Thomas Allen as art director of the company. A year later Alfred and Louise Powell had a series of designs accepted by the company, and the couple's influence shortly resulted in a new school of free-hand painting being founded at Etruria. In 1906 Kennard left for the United States to represent the company's interests there.

Daisy Makeig-Jones applied directly to Cecil Wedgwood in 1909 and gained employment as an apprentice painter. Her ostentatious "Fairyland Lustre" designs of the 1920s were well received by a British public tired of wartime austerity, but sadly

10

Earthenware plaque painted by Thomas Allen with a Nubian woman within an "Isis" border, 1878.

11

"Fairyland Lustre" plate decorated with the "Imps on a Bridge and Tree House" pattern designed by Daisy Makeig-Jones, 1920s[1] (OPPOSITE).

12

"Persephone" pattern plate, designed by Eric Ravilious in 1938.

Cecil did not live to see this phenomenon – he lost his life in World War I. His daughter, Doris Audrey Wedgwood, took his place on the Wedgwood board of directors until her retirement in 1928. Meanwhile, in New York, Kennard had founded a subsidiary American company that was named Josiah Wedgwood & Sons Inc in 1919.

Francis Hamilton Wedgwood served as a recruitment officer at Lichfield Barracks, Staffordshire, during World War I and was therefore able to maintain close contact with Etruria throughout the hostilities. After the war, he became chairman and managing director, and employed Norman Wilson as works manager. Wilson oversaw the instal-

---

JOHN EDWARD GOODWIN (1867–1949)

John Goodwin joined the design staff at Etruria in 1892 and was appointed art director in 1904. This was a time of great rationalization for Wedgwood and Goodwin proved a realistic manager. He replaced the Victorian-inspired art wares with more conventional ranges and adapted many of Wedgwood's original 18th-century tableware shapes and patterns to suit 20th-century demands. Goodwin particularly targeted the American market, which had traditionally

always admired Wedgwood's wares in the "Federal" (neo-classical) style.
An ideal balance was formed at Wedgwood, with Goodwin overseeing the manufacture of commercial ornamental wares (by designers such as Daisy Makeig-Jones) and Alfred and Louise Powell concentrating on art wares.
Before his retirement in 1934, Goodwin's marketing experience with traditional middle-range tableware helped Wedgwood to survive the disastrous effects of the Depression.

ALFRED HOARE POWELL (1865–1960)
ADA LOUISE POWELL (1882–1956)

In 1903 Wedgwood received a series of contemporary designs from Alfred Powell and, conscious of the public interest generated by the Arts and Crafts Movement, immediately realized their potential and put them into production. Powell trained as an architect, but in the 1890s abandoned the traditions of "drawing board" design and became involved with the revival of vernacular styles. In 1906 he married Emile Lessore's granddaughter, Ada Louise, and the couple began working together as Alfred H and Louise Powell. Early in the following year Wedgwood set up a studio for them at Bloomsbury, in London.
Louise Powell trained at the Central School of Art in London, and was for many years closely associated with the Arts and Crafts Exhibition Society. She and her husband often worked together on important commissions and it is therefore sometimes difficult to distinguish the individual hand. Their designs tend to fall into two categories: either fairly simple flower and foliage sprig patterns for tableware or rich Islamic- and Renaissance-inspired pictorial, foliate, and armorial designs for ornamental pieces.
The Powells visited Etruria regularly, and on one occasion forwarded the idea of producing some existing printed and painted tableware patterns in a totally free-hand form. This met with approval and a number of such patterns were retailed through the firm of James Powell & Sons, to whose owner Alfred was related. This successful revival of hand-painting at Etruria led to the establishment of the handcraft department, under Millicent Taplin, during the 1920s. The volume of work that Alfred and Louise Powell executed for Wedgwood declined after Francis Wedgwood's death in 1930, but the couple continued to purchase blanks from Etruria. Much of their later work comprised armorial chargers for country house owners and depictions of historic buildings.

lation of the factory's first gas-fired glost tunnel-oven in 1927. Francis Hamilton died suddenly two years later and was succeeded as managing director by his nephew, The Hon Josiah Wedgwood (Josiah V), the great-great-great-grandson of the firm's founder. Josiah V was aided at Etruria by his cousins, Clement Tom Wedgwood and Sir John Hamilton Wedgwood. Another cousin, Hensleigh, moved to New York in 1931 and became president of the American branch until his retirement in 1960.

The economic slump following the Wall Street Crash of 1929 caused hardships at Etruria, and Josiah V was forced to take stringent economical measures in order to keep Wedgwood afloat. However, morale

MILLICENT JANE TAPLIN (1902–80)

Under the influence of Alfred and Louise Powell, girls from various art schools began to be trained at Etruria in free-hand pottery decoration. Initially, Alfred ("Beaver") Powell gave them drawing lessons, and only after several months' training were they allowed to progress to the overglaze painting of earthenware. By the mid-1920s the girls were hard at work on the Powells' Queen's ware designs and in 1826 a handcraft painting studio was opened under the supervision of Millicent Taplin.
Taplin began working for Wedgwood in 1917, when she was still a part-time student at the Stoke and Burslem Schools of Art. She became involved in the painting of Persian and Rhodian wares (see Earthenware) and was selected to train under Powell. In 1928 she started to create her own patterns and by the late 1930s had become one of Wedgwood's most productive designers.
During World War II, Taplin took up full-time teaching at the Stoke School of Art, but remained a consultant for Wedgwood and returned to Etruria when peace prevailed. From about 1956 to her retirement in 1962 she ran the newly combined china and earthenware hand-painting departments.

remained high and the company's image was boosted during the depressed 1930s, not only by celebrations of the bicentennial of Josiah I's birth, but also by the commissioning of work from successful outside designers, such as Keith Murray and Eric Ravilious. The tradition of commissioning external artists had been begun by Josiah I, who utilized contemporaries such as John Flaxman, John Bacon, and George Stubbs. In 1934 Victor Skellern succeeded John Goodwin as art director.

Meanwhile, the Etruria factory was fast proving inadequate for modern manufacturing methods and was also physically subsiding because of the close proximity of mining operations. In 1936 Josiah V announced the momentous decision to move the company to a new rural location. After much invest-

igation, a suitable 380-acre (154-hectare) site was found at unpolluted Barlaston, an area that had previously been home to many Wedgwood family members, including Sarah (Josiah I's widow) and Francis (from 1848).

Barlaston

. . . the Wedgwood tradition prescribes a duty to the future as well as to the past generations . . .
(FROM JOSIAH V'S PRESS RELEASE OF MAY 1936.)

Keith Murray, in his architectural partnership with Charles S. White, was chosen to design the new works. Louis de Soisson, architect of Welwyn Garden City in Hertfordshire, was selected to set out a custom-

13

Mat green glazed vase, one of many functional wares designed by Keith Murray in the 1930s.

KEITH DAY PEARCE MURRAY (1892–1981)

Born in New Zealand, Keith Murray moved with his family to England in about 1906. He served with distinction in the Royal Flying Corps during World War II, and afterwards trained as an architect, but found it impossible to obtain work in the depressed financial climate. As a result he began to take an interest in contemporary glass design and in 1932 he was engaged at the Stevens and Williams Glassworks in Brierly Hill. In the same year, Wedgwood first used his freelance services and within a matter of months he was secured to work for the company on a regular basis.

Murray rapidly developed a series of simple, functional tableware and vases incorporating Wedgwood's newly developed mat opaque glazes (see Mat Glazes), as well as traditional bodies such as black basaltes and red stoneware. The range was exhibited in London and on the Continent from 1933 to 1937 and was well received. Most of his designs were included in Wedgwood's Catalogue of Glazes, Bodies and Shapes Current for 1940–1950 and many were still being produced well into the 1950s. His last major ceramic design task for Wedgwood came in 1946 – a completely new table service combining plain utilitarian appeal with the capacity to carry any form of decoration. Not surprisingly, the "Commonwealth" service took two years, and a large production team, to complete.

During 1938 a foundation stone was laid at the site of Keith Murray's largest physical achievement for Wedgwood. In his capacity as an architect he was selected to design, with his partner Charles S White, the modern factory at Barlaston.

CECILY STELLA ("STAR") WEDGWOOD (1904-   )

Star, the daughter of Francis Hamilton (Major Frank) Wedgwood, was introduced to pottery decoration in the late 1920s by way of Alfred Powell's painting classes at Etruria. During the early 1930s she became a designer herself and was responsible for a number of patterns on bone china and Queen's ware. In 1937 she married Frederick Maitland Wright, who later became Wedgwood's company secretary and joint managing director with Norman Wilson.

NORMAN WILSON (1902-85)

The son of a china manufacturer, Norman Wilson spent the early 1920s at the North Staffordshire Technical College. When his father's health began to suffer, Wilson found himself running the family business as well as continuing his studies. Growing tired of the continuous struggle, he emigrated to Canada and began to earn a living breaking ponies.

In 1927 he was contacted by Francis Hamilton Wedgwood and returned home to replace Major Bernard Moore as works manager at Etruria. He supervised the installation of new kilns and developed various bodies and new mat glazes. His design work included new tableware shapes, such as "Barlaston" (modeled by Eric Owen), "Globe," and "Leigh."

After serving in World War II he was appointed production director at Barlaston in 1946, and from 1961 until his retirement in 1963 he served as joint managing director with Frederick Maitland Wright. Throughout his career with Wedgwood, Wilson produced a number of "Unique" studio wares (see Commemorative Wares), which were not designed to be retailed through the normal channels. A selection of these were shown at the Grafton Galleries in 1936 (see Victor George Skellern).

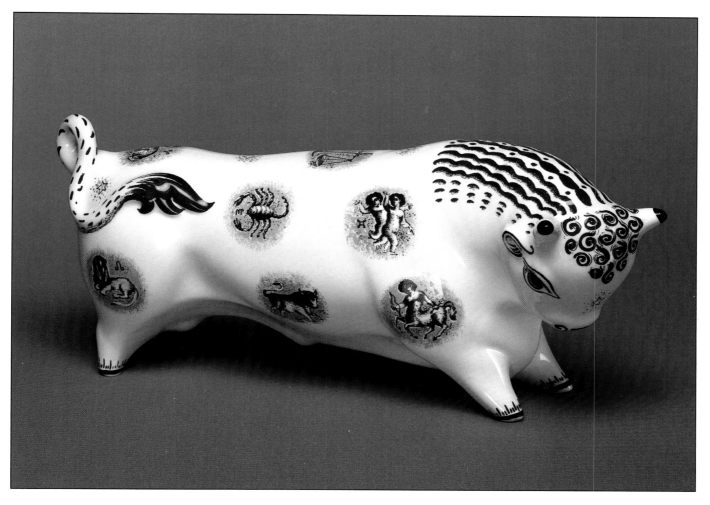

built workers' village on the estate. A founda-tion-stone laying ceremony took place in September 1938, and earthenware production at Barlaston began two years later. However, the outbreak of World War II in 1939 halted the ambitious housing project and interrupted building work at the factory. Thus, biscuit bone china continued to be made at Etruria until 1947, although it was glazed in the cleaner atmosphere at Barlaston. Josiah I's old factory finally closed in 1950, by which time all manufacturing processes had been transferred to the new works.

During World War II, all output of decor-ated ware for the home market was suspended and replaced by simple white "Utility" ware. However, the export of expensive decorative ware to North America was still permitted, and indeed encouraged by the British government as a way of off-setting any financial aid they might seek from across the Atlantic.

14

Figure of "Taurus" modeled by Arnold Machin and printed and painted with Eric Ravilious' "Zodiac" pattern, 1945. This model is still in production today.

ARNOLD MACHIN (1911–)

Born and educated in the Potteries, Machin joined Minton as an apprentice painter while also studying modeling at the Stoke School of Art. During the Depression he left to work for Royal Crown Derby and then became a student at the Derby School of Art, later winning a scholarship to the Royal College of Art. In 1940 he was employed as a full-time figure modeler at Barlaston, where he spent the war years producing figures and groups in a manner reminiscent of traditional Staffordshire "flat-backs."
In the 1950s Machin taught at art schools in both Stoke and London. During the 1960s he designed new coinage and was awarded the honor of an OBE in 1964 for his work in this field.

Fortunately, Wedgwood's New York branch was already well established and could play an important promotional role for its parent company. A set of 12 plates showing "Old London Views" was issued in North America, along with a leaflet explaining Wedgwood's two-fold aim of aiding the British people (a third of the sale profits being donated to the British War Relief Society) and of providing the owner with "a lasting memento of their contribution to the British cause."

Arnold Machin, who first designed for Wedgwood in 1940, spent the war years at Barlaston as a conscientious objector. During that time, he modeled bas-relief portraits of Churchill and Roosevelt, which were incorporated into designs for patriotic mugs with the accompanying inscriptions, "Give us the tools and we will finish the job" and "It can be done, it must be done, it shall be done!"

After the war, Norman Wilson became production director at Barlaston. Wedgwood's Canadian and Australian companies were formed in 1948 and 1955, respectively. Clement Tom Wedgwood retired and emigrated to Rhodesia in 1951. Richard Guyatt became consultant designer for three years from 1952 and work was commissioned from Laurence Whistler in 1955–56. A much scaled-down Barlaston housing estate was completed by the late 1950s.

Expansion

But once you've moved, and once you've got a new factory, it's all go, let's get bigger, let's do better.

(BERT LOWE, ACCOUNTANT AT ETRURIA AND BARLASTON.)

Josiah V retired as managing director in 1964 and was replaced by Sir Arthur Bryan, a Staffordshire-born man who was previously the firm's New York president. The tradition of family control at Wedgwood ended three years later when Sir Arthur became chairman. The year 1966 marked the retirement of Sir John Hamilton Wedgwood and the first acquisitions of rival manufacturing companies – to form the Wedgwood Group. Clement Tom Wedgwood's son, Alan, joined the company in the same year; he became the

sole descendant of Josiah I on the board of directors.

Wedgwood registered as a public company in 1967 and its shares were launched on the stock market. In the same year, Richard Guyatt again became consultant designer. A new Wedgwood Museum was opened at Barlaston in 1969 by Lord Clark, former director of the National Gallery, London. Eduardo Paolozzi designed a limited-edition set of six striking silk-screen plates in 1970. The "Egyptian Collection" was issued in 1978 and Robert Minkin became art director in 1979. The following year marked the 250th anniversary of the birth of Josiah I and the bicentennial of Thomas Bentley's death.

In the 20 years since its inception, the Wedgwood Group had taken over many well-known local ceramic firms, including William Adams, Coalport, Susie Cooper, Crown Staffordshire, Johnson Brothers, Mason's Ironstone, J & G Meakin, and Midwinter. After a hostile bid from London International plc, the Group was itself taken over by Waterford Glass Group plc in November 1986 and was renamed "Waterford Wedgwood" in 1989.

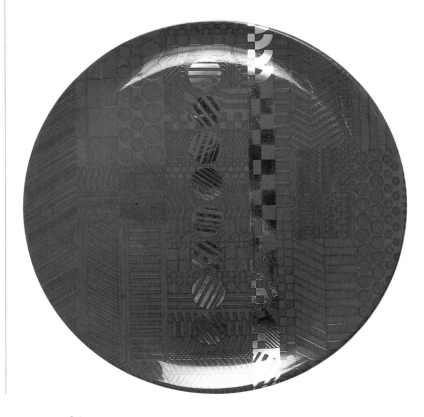

WALTER ROBERT MINKIN (1928–   )

Robert Minkin trained at the Wimbledon College of Art and the Royal College of Art. He joined Wedgwood as chief designer in 1955 and progressed to design director by 1979. As well as producing a number of distinctive tableware patterns, he is renowned for a cylindrical coffee set that was first issued in black basaltes and later in ravenstone mat glaze. Minkin was also responsible for the gilt plaques, adapted from originals in the Tutankhamun treasure, which formed part of the 1978 "Egyptian Collection." He retired in 1989.

EDUARDO LUIGI PAOLOZZI (1928–   )

Paolozzi studied at the College of Art in his home town of Edinburgh before training at the Slade School of Fine Art, Oxford and London. Thereafter he lectured at various art institutions, both national and international, and his work achieved many awards. In 1970 he designed a limited-edition set of six brightly coloured silk-screen printed plates for Wedgwood, entitled "Variations on a Geometric Theme."

15

Two silk-screen printed bone china plates from the "Variations on a Geometric Theme" set designed by Eduardo Paolozzi, 1970.

The Wedgwood Ceramic Range

16

Black basaltes "Canopic" jar with encaustic decoration, *c*. The form is derived from funerary jars used by the ancient Egyptians and Etruscans.

This is divided into three sections – Stoneware, Earthenware, and Porcelain. Specific materials and styles are arranged alphabetically within each section.

Stoneware

Stoneware pottery is fired to a very high temperature (above 1200°C/2192°F), at which point it vitrifies and becomes impervious to liquid.

WHITE SALT-GLAZED STONEWARE (*c*1752 TO PRE-1764)

A method of glazing stoneware with volatilized common salt was established in China in the Chou Dynasty (1110–256 BC) and had been adopted in Europe by at least the 15th century. When salt is introduced into a red-hot kiln it breaks down into its two components, sodium and chlorine. The sodium combines with the alumina and silica in the clay to form a wafer-thin clear coating with minute "orange-peel" pitting, which allows the crispness of any relief decoration to be fully retained. The noxious chlorinated fumes are ejected through the kiln flue.

Finely pitted refined stoneware, whitened with powdered calcined flint and often additionally dipped in a white pipeclay slip, became a staple product of the Staffordshire

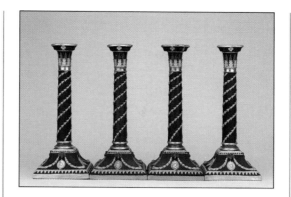

potters in the mid-18th century. Salt-glazed wares were made by the Wedgwood, Harrison and Alders partnership, and Josiah I stated that during his period with Thomas Whieldon "White stoneware was the principal article of our manufacture." Wedgwood also continued production for some time at the Ivy House works.

Dry-body Stoneware

BLACK BASALTES (FROM 1768)

While at the Brick House works, Josiah Wedgwood I developed a refined black stoneware derived from the coarse unglazed

17

Set of four gilt black basaltes candlesticks in the form of Corinthian

18

White salt-glazed stoneware jug and cover, with applied ornament, *c*1755 (BELOW LEFT).

19

Black basaltes "Herculaneum Subject" roundel, showing traces of original gilding, *c*1774. Such plaques were used as architectural features, and were inspired by Roman wall paintings reproduced in *Le Antichita di Ercolano Esposte*, published by order of the King of Naples and Sicily, the future Charles III of Spain.

"black Egyptian" pottery that was made by the Wedgwood-Whieldon partnership and by many other Staffordshire potters. By 1768 he had successfully modified the existing fabric to withstand high-temperature firings. The new dense body, originally called "Etruscan," could either be left in its natural satin finish, polished to a high gloss on a lapidary wheel, or "bronzed" with a fine coating of lightly fired powdered gold. It could also be decorated with engine-turned patterns, bas-relief work, or encaustic painting. By 1773 Wedgwood had renamed his

20

Silver-mounted black basaltes fox's-head stirrup cup, c1775.

Etruscan ware "black basaltes," after the hard black igneous rock that was much sculpted by the Egyptians.

Wedgwood's 1779 *Ornamental Catalogue* lists a diversity of black basaltes products: "Cameos and Intaglios . . . Busts, Small Statues . . . Antique Vases (highly finished with bas-relief ornaments) . . . Painted Etruscan Vases . . . Tablets and pictures for cabinets – from Bracelet size to pieces of Eighteen or Twenty inches Diameter." The material was also used for tea ware, inkwells, lamps, bulb pots, and other objects.

A range of black basaltes wares, decorated with *famille rose*-style translucent enamels, was introduced in 1810. A dark chocolate-

---

JOHN FLAXMAN, SR (1726–95)
JOHN FLAXMAN, JR (1755–1826)

(Father and son initially worked together as modelers and casters, so it can prove difficult to differentiate their individual work for Wedgwood with any certainty.)

Flaxman, Jr, was a frail child who spent most of his early years drawing and reading at his father's shop in Covent Garden, London. As his modeling talents improved he naturally began to assist his father and firmly established his worth by designing a medal for which he was awarded the first prize of the Society of Arts in 1767. Soon afterward he enrolled at the Academy Schools, where his work was exhibited in 1770. Five years later he was commissioned by Wedgwood, but it is apparent that Flaxman, Sr, had already established a business relationship some years previously.

For over a decade Flaxman, Jr, produced an exhaustive selection of busts, figures, portrait medallions, bas-relief work, chessmen, and other objects for Wedgwood. He set up on his own account in 1782 and in 1787 went to Rome, where he was partly financed by Wedgwood to further his studies and to supervise the copying of antique friezes. Seven years later he returned to London to concentrate on monumental sculpture, although he did also produce a small amount of further work for Wedgwood. He was elected a Member of the Royal Academy in 1800.

21

Pair of black basaltes wine and water ewers c1778. The models were supplied by John Flaxman, Sr, in 1775.

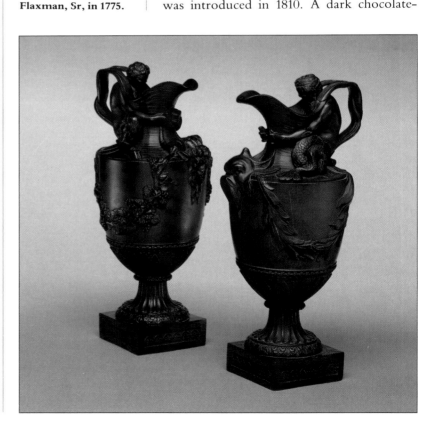

GEORGE STUBBS (1724–1806)

The famous British painter began experimenting with fired enamels on copper in about 1769, but found the necessarily small supports too restraining. In 1775 he contacted Thomas Bentley regarding ceramic blanks and, in response, Josiah Wedgwood attempted to make earthenware biscuit plaques of a suitable size. In May 1779 he reported successful firings of large tablets. These proved expensive; to offset the cost, Stubbs went to Etruria Hall for three months in 1780 to paint the Wedgwood family.

Many blanks were produced for Stubbs, in a variety of sizes, up until Josiah I's death, and it was hoped that the artist's fired work would be as well received as his oils, thus encouraging other painters to follow suit. However, although technically successful, the finished products were publicly considered unworthy. Many such pieces remained unsold at Stubbs's studio until his death, when they were auctioned for wildly varying prices. Stubbs's only recorded sculptural works are the Frightened Horse *and* Fall of Phaeton *plaques, modeled at Etruria and issued in both black basaltes and jasperware.*

brown stoneware, almost identical to black basaltes, with rich gilt relief ornamentation was produced for a short period from *c*1880. Ernest William Light, a well-known sculptor in the Potteries (and later Master-in-Charge of the Stoke School of Art), was commissioned to design a series of black basaltes animal and bird models in 1913. The medium also suited many of Keith Murray's pure forms of the 1930s.

22

Two black basaltes busts, of Mercury (*left*) and Minerva (*right*), 19th century.

23

A 19th-century version of George Stubb's black basaltes *Frightened Horse* plaque, modeled in 1780.

24

Black basaltes "Fish Tail" or "Stella" ewer, *c*1775. The design is taken from Jacques de Stella's *Livre de Vases aux Galeries de Louvre.* Josiah I referred to such pieces as "Stella's ewers."

CANE WARE (FROM c1770)

"Cane ware," whose color can actually vary from tan-yellow to buff, was the result of Josiah Wedgwood I's refinement of common Staffordshire iron-bearing brown pottery. Having experienced many difficulties with his early cane-colored body, satisfactory results were only obtained after further trials by his son, Josiah II, in 1783. Cane ware first appeared in the 1787 catalog as "bamboo" ware and was indeed the ideal medium for Wedgwood's Oriental-inspired bamboo-form flower holders, jugs, tea ware, and other items. Such pieces, bearing enameled details and borders, were very popular and were made in great quantity at the end of the 18th century.

The deprivations caused in Britain by the wheat famines of the late 18th and early 19th centuries provided Wedgwood with the ideal opportunity promoting a coarser cane-colored body which was molded to simulate pastry cases and pie crusts. *Famille rose*-decorated cane ware was introduced in the early 19th century in the same shape range as the enameled black basaltes wares that were being produced at the time.

(*See also* Cane ware *in the* Earthenware section below.)

25

Cane ware (stoneware) game pie dish, colored and relief-decorated to simulate pastry, c1850 (ABOVE).

26

Cane ware (stoneware) bamboo-molded early morning tea set (solitaire) with encaustic painted borders, c1800 (BELOW).

DRAB WARE
(EARLY 19TH CENTURY TO c1860)

Finely pitted salt-glazed stoneware vessels with dull olive-gray "drab ware" bodies and white details were produced in Staffordshire from the 1720s onwards. Wedgwood revived this drab color in the early 19th century, first in dry-body stoneware and then in glazed earthenware. Drab stoneware was mainly used for decorative pieces, relieved with contrasting ornamentation, although occasionally it appeared as bas-relief work on cane ware. The color was never very popular and was withdrawn by c1860.

27

Drab ware (stoneware)
Gothic-style jug,
c1830.

28

18th-century
jasperware mounted as
jewelry, and a
mounted scent bottle.
The cut steel mounts
were probably made
by Matthew Boulton
in Birmingham.

JASPERWARE (FROM 1774)

American clay was used in Britain as early as the mid-1740s during initial attempts to manufacture porcelain. Josiah Wedgwood I's efforts to produce a completely new ceramic body began in the mid-1760s with experiments on clay dug from beds lying in Cherokee Indian country, but the supply of this raw material proved difficult and expensive. In 1771 he recommenced experiments in earnest and, after thousands of trials, discovered three years later that barium sulphate, obtainable from Derbyshire barium (known locally as "cawk"), provided the vital missing ingredient for his formula. The resulting high-fired, dense, white stoneware body was easily tinted with a variety of colors, held very sharp detail and could be decorated with bas-relief work of a contrasting color. Initial manufacturing problems were generally overcome by November 1775, when Wedgwood began referring to his new product as "jasper" with some confidence.

In December 1777 Wedgwood suggested to Bentley that jasper should be promoted as being made of Cherokee clay, which was obtained with the "utmost difficulty," but later in the same letter he ambiguously stated that only "a portion of the Cherokee clay is really used in all the jaspers." In the same year, dipped backgrounds were introduced, with a thin coating of colored jasper being applied over a white base. "Jasper-dip"

MATTHEW BOULTON (1728–1809)

Boulton was the chief decorative metalwork manufacturer in 18th-century England and, like Josiah Wedgwood I, was a major contributor to the Industrial Revolution. He opened the Soho Engineering Workshops at Birmingham in 1765 and Josiah became a frequent visitor and admirer of his equipment and products. The idea of mounting Wedgwood's vases in Boulton's French-style ormolu was mutually discussed but did not come to fruition. The two men respected each other as friendly rivals and Josiah eventually supplied Boulton with jasperware cameos for mounting as jewelry.

29

Jasperware plaque depicting Erato, the Muse of love poetry, attributed to William Hackwood, c1778.

30

Jasperware chess pieces from a set designed by Arnold Machin in 1938.

31 **32**

Two unusual jasperware vases: a "Quiver" vase (lacking cover), *c*1790; a "Viola da Gamba" vase, intended to "captivate musical people" and first produced in 1801 (BELOW).

33

Jasperware chess pieces
from a set modeled by
John Flaxman, Jr, in
1784, dating from
*c*1790. (ABOVE).

34

Two examples of
intricate three-color
jasperware, with
"Aurora in her
Chariot" central
motifs, *c*1980.

Jasperware Art Deco "Sun and Wind" plaque, designed by Anna Zinkeisen in 1924. This example is dated 1957.

ANNA KATRINA ZINKEISEN (1906–78)

While studying sculpture at the Royal Academy Schools, Zinkeisen was commissioned by Wedgwood to design three jasperware plaques – "Adam," "Eve," and "Sun and Wind." The first two were awarded a silver medal at the 1925 Paris Exposition, and all three plaques were reissued at various later dates in the 20th century.

Zinkeisen was a war artist and also painted murals on the passenger ships Queen Mary *and* Queen Elizabeth.

grounds were cheaper, as less coloring pigment was necessary, and they also reduced any tendency to bleed.

When first produced, jasper was reserved only for small seals, cameos, and medallions as the bas-relief ornaments tended to lift and buckle on a large, curved surface. But experimental work with small objects such as candlesticks, bowls, and lamps eventually led to successes with large ornamental pieces. Blue and white proved the most popular jasper color combination in the 18th century and has remained so until the present day. The early solid blue body was reintroduced in 1854 and has stayed in production ever since. Solid "Royal" blue was introduced to celebrate the coronation of Elizabeth II in 1953 and "Portland" blue first appeared in the range in 1972.

A mainstream production of traditional classical-style jasper has been adhered to over the centuries, but expanding demands and increasing production costs have led to reductions in quality. Contemporary jasper designs have met with limited success, but the Art Nouveau-style foliate patterns of Harry Barnard and the Art Deco plaques by Anna Zinkeisen are notable.

36

Jasperware bell pulls, designed to be hung from a sash or cord, c1790. Scent bottles were produced in much the same form.

37

Jasperware "Homeric Vase," ornamented with the "Apotheosis of Homer" (modeled by John Flaxman, Jr), the cover with a Pegasus finial, c1786.

JASPERWARE COLORS

black	dip – 1778–1854 with reduced quantities thereafter solid – for bas-relief work, and for small ornamental pieces in the 20th century
crimson	dip only – 1910 and 1925–32 (discontinued due to color bleeding)
green	dip – sage green 1778–1854, dark olive green 1920–30 solid – sage green 1775–78, reintroduced 1957
lilac	dip – 1778–1854 solid – originally only for bas-relief work, full production 1960–62
primrose yellow	solid – introduced 1976
terracotta	solid – for bas-relief work from 1775, full production 1957–59
turquoise	dip – 1875 to c1885
yellow buff	dip – yellow from 1778 in small quantities solid – with black, bas-relief work 1929–33

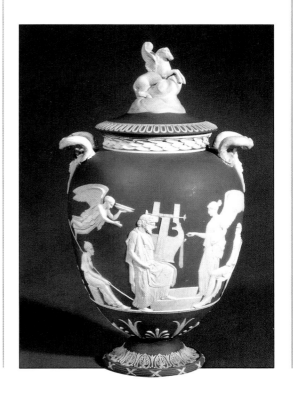

38

Two *rosso antico* vases, the bodies dipped in black basaltes slip and then engine turned to show the ground color, c1780–85.

39

Jasperware "Choice (Judgment) of Hercules" plaque modeled by William Hackwood, c1777.

RED STONEWARE (FROM c1760)

Unglazed red stoneware (generally unmarked other than with impressed pseudo-Chinese seal marks) was made in imitation of Chinese Yixing ware by numerous mid-18th-century Staffordshire potters. Josiah I soon became dissatisfied with his once best-selling red tea-pots and "commonest wares," finding them vulgar and cheap, and it was only at Bentley's insistence that a new stoneware body was introduced in 1776. This was similar in color to Roman red ware (*terra Sigillata*) and was marketed under the name of *"rosso antico"* (antique red).

Josiah I never really lost his old prejudices against red stoneware and *rosso antico* was not popularized until the early 19th century

40

Rosso antico bust of
George II. The 1773
Wedgwood catalog
lists a bust of George II
"from an ivory in the
possession of Mr
Ranby, carved by Mr
Rysbrack."

41

Black basaltes
Egyptian-taste coffee
pot with *rosso antico*
decoration, the finial
formed as a crocodile,
late 18th century.

alongside a slightly coarser "terracotta" ware. From 1810 Wedgwood's red stoneware, like black basaltes and cane ware, was often painted with *famille rose* enamels.

WHITE BISCUIT WARE (MAINLY 19TH CENTURY)

A limited amount of white biscuit (unglazed) stoneware was made by Josiah I in the form of plant pots with engine-turned stripes of coloured slip. It is a much softer and less compact body than white jasper (with which it is sometimes confused) and, like *rosso antico*, was popularized in Josiah II's period. Examples from the 19th century are normally ornamented with contrasting relief work, in the manner of jasper, and are frequently thinly "smear-glazed" by the volatilization of a glaze preparation smeared on the inside of the saggar (the box in which the piece is fired).

Stoneware mortar and pestle, c1780. A general interest in science led Josiah I to introduce a range of chemical stonewares ("mortar ware") in 1779.

Earthenware

Earthenware pottery is not fired to the point of vitrification and therefore requires glazing in order to become functional. Glazes can be transparent, translucent, or opaque, depending on requirement, and are normally applied either by dipping or spraying. Tin-glazed earthenware, which was common in Britain up until the early 19th century, was not produced by Josiah Wedgwood I.

AGATE WARE (FROM c1754)

SOLID AGATE Many mid-18th-century Staffordshire potters, including the Wedgwood-Whieldon partnership, produced useful wares that were made in imitation of striated natural hardstones by press-molding or throwing local dark clays wedged (layered) with West Country white pipeclay. The marbling of these "solid" agate wares extends throughout the body and is often very finely detailed. In 1759 Josiah I recorded that he had "already made an imitation of Agate which was esteemed beautiful," but added that "people were surfeited with wares of these various

colors" and turned his attention mainly to surface agate patterning.

SURFACE AGATE A similar effect to solid agate can be obtained by painting the surface of cream-colored earthenware with colored clay slips. While the result is somewhat coarser and less dramatic, there is less tendency for the colors to merge together.

Costly classical-style hardstone vases were *de rigueur* in the fashionable interiors of Robert Adam's time. The pottery copies supplied by Wedgwood and Bentley provided a convincing and cheap alternative for those who were suffering from what Josiah I referred to as "vase madness."

ANNULAR WARE (INTRODUCED c1933)

A new tableware shape in a distinctive horizontally ridged modernistic style was designed in the early 1930s by Clement Tom Wedgwood and John Goodwin, with assistance from Keith Murray and in co-operation with the retailer, Rouard of Paris. "Annular" ware was decorated with the newly introduced mat glazes.

ARGENTA WARE (1879 TO c1900)

In an attempt to bring majolica up-to-date, a new range of ornamental forms was brought out by Wedgwood after 1878 with predominantly pale backgrounds. These were purposely Oriental in manner in order to capitalize on the influence of Japanese art that swept Europe in the late 19th century.

CANE WARE (20TH CENTURY)

Inspired by cane-colored stoneware (*see also* Stoneware), self-colored glazed cane earthenware bodies were made by Wedgwood in the 20th century and were marketed under various names such as "Honey-Buff" tableware (made for the London retailers Heals in 1930 and reintroduced as "Cane" in 1956/57) and "Harvest Moon" (first issued in the 1930s).

CELADON WARE (FROM 1805)

The term "celadon" was given to Chinese stoneware with a characteristic grayish-green glaze. Wedgwood introduced a successful self-colored clear-glazed earthenware body in 1805 in imitation of celadon.

43

Queen's ware jelly molds, c1790. The plain hollow molds were inverted and filled with gelatinous dessert and the decorated wedges fitted inside. When the dessert was set, the covers were removed and the decoration was visible through the jelly (ABOVE).

44

Agate ware vase (*right*) and porphyry vase (*left*), both c1775 (OPPOSITE).

45

Queen's ware foot bath, c1800. These utilitarian vessels are now sought after for use as jardinières.

CREAM-COLORED EARTHENWARE (FROM c1761)

The transportation of white West Country clays to the north of England from the 1720s onward enabled the Staffordshire potters to produce a cream-colored earthenware that was previously only possible by covering a dark fabric with a cream slip. Early "cream-ware" was made from the same body as white salt-glazed stoneware, but was fired at a lower temperature and coated with a clear glaze containing powdered lead ore (galena) and ground flint. Initially, the glaze was

46

Creamware teapot decorated with a "Chintz" pattern in the manner associated with David Rhodes, c1770.

DAVID RHODES (D 1777)

During the 1760s, many creamware manufacturers began employing the services of specialist "outside" decorators. Josiah Wedgwood I entered into an arrangement with the firm of Jasper Robinson and David Rhodes, of Leeds, for the supply of copper scales (used as the coloring ingredient for his green glaze) and at the same time sold them plain creamware for enameling. Robinson relinquished his partnership in 1763 but continued to work for Rhodes until the latter's apparent departure five years later.

In 1768 Josiah I took the lease of a house on St Martin's Lane, London, and engaged a "Master Enameller and China piecer . . . just come out of Yorkshire" with whom he had previous connections: this was presumably Rhodes. Within a week, Wedgwood had selected alternative premises, at No 1 Great Newport Street, and soon installed his tenant there. Rhodes later moved to the Chelsea Decorating Studio, where he worked as master enameler and oversaw the decoration of the "Frog" service for Catherine the Great.

47

Selection of 18th-century Wedgwood Queen's ware for the table.

dusted on and the objects were given only one firing. However, the dry ingredients proved harmful to the potters and a safer fluid glaze was developed in *c*1740. This necessitated a double firing – first to a biscuit stage and then, once dipped, to the glazed state. Eventually all creamware was double-fired in this manner.

By 1761 Josiah Wedgwood I was directing all his efforts toward the improvement of creamware and two years later he achieved a paler, lightweight fabric. Both body and glaze were further transformed in 1768 to a degree that virtually created a new product. Royal patronage resulted in the name "Queen's ware" being applied to Wedgwood's creamware and Josiah I successfully targeted both the English and Continental aristocracy, deliberately pricing his cream-colored earthenware artificially high in order to place it alongside fine porcelain. This marketing ploy was perfectly timed as Queen's ware was brought to the fore just at the moment when the rococo style was yielding to the neoclassical, shifting the ceramic taste of the cognoscenti away from porcelain and toward pottery. Only when trade had been

48

Queen's ware mug, overglaze-prnted with a hunting scene, a typical Sadler and Green print, *c*1770.

49

Queen's ware three-tier set of stacking meat pans, and a combined night lamp and tea warmer (*veilleuse*), *c*1850.

JOHN SADLER (1720–89)
GUY GREEN (FL 1750–99)

On July 27, 1756, John Sadler, with the sole assistance of Guy Green, reputedly printed an impressive 1,200 delftware tiles in six hours in Liverpool, using the transfer technique (see Processes of Manufacture). Sadler claimed to have invented this method but, while he may have genuinely discovered it independently, it is more likely that he adapted a process that was already in fairly common use by 1755.

An account in respect of printing creamware for Wedgwood was opened in September 1761, by which time Sadler had taken Green into partial partnership. Recognizing the vast national and international potential for cheaply decorated printed wares, Josiah I absorbed as much as possible of the printing firm's work capacity in order to try and prevent any acceptance of orders from other manufacturers. Liaisons continually took place over design subjects, and an arrangement was made whereby the printers could actually purchase plain creamware from Wedgwood for decorating and selling on their own account in Liverpool.

John Sadler retired in 1770 and handed over the business to his partner. Guy Green continued to print for Wedgwood until 1795, and retired four years later.

firmly established did Josiah consider dropping the prices of his Queen's ware.

Cream-colored earthenware may be left "in the white," generally with relief-molded or pierced decoration; it can be colored with underglaze oxides (*see* Tortoise-shell Ware) or tinted glazes; it can also be painted with enamel colors or transfer printed over the glaze (*see* Printed Wares). Much of Josiah I's enameling was undertaken by David Rhodes, while Sadler and Green were contracted as his printers. By the end of the 18th century the amount of exported fine quality English creamware was immense: its manufacture was necessarily adopted by European potters who realized that their traditional livelihood from tin-glazed wares was under threat.

DRAB WARE (EARLY 19TH CENTURY TO *c*1860)

A glazed earthenware body, ranging in color from pale coffee to dark olive, was introduced at about the same time as celadon ware and was mainly reserved for useful tablewares. The interiors of such pieces were frequently washed in contrasting white or robin's egg blue. Drab earthenware, like its stoneware counterpart, was never very popular and was withdrawn by *c*1860. It did, however, enjoy a revival in the 1970s through special orders for Tiffany's of New York.

(*See also* Stoneware.)

JOHN RATTENBURY SKEAPING
(1901–80)

Son of the painter Kenneth Mathieson Skeaping, John Skeaping studied at several London art schools, including the Royal Academy, and was awarded the Prix de Rome in 1924. He was taught to carve marble in Rome and married the sculptor Barbara Hepworth, who had a profound influence on his work (the marriage was dissolved in 1933). In 1926 he was commissioned to model a series of animal studies for Wedgwood, which he designed in a contemporary economic style. The figures were issued in plain black basaltes and Queen's ware and also with a variety of mat glazes. Many remained in production throughout the 1930s, some were still being made in the 1950s, and a few models were reissued as late as 1959. Skeaping traveled widely and continued to concentrate on animal subjects, many in connection with horse racing. He became a Royal Academician in 1959.

50

"Moonstone" glazed figure of a sea lion, one of a number of animal studies modeled by John Skeaping in 1926 and 1927.

51

Cauliflower-molded
teapot, c1760-65. The
leaves are picked out
in the translucent
green glaze perfected
by Josiah Wedgwood I
in 1759.

52

Drab ware
(earthenware) cup and
saucer with raised
"Prunus" relief, the
cup interior washed in
contrasting pale
"robin's egg" blue,
c1820.

FRUIT AND VEGETABLE
MOLDED WARE (FROM c1760)

Porcelain articles molded in the form of fruit
and vegetables, and painted in naturalistic
colors, proved popular during the rococo
period and caused Josiah Wedgwood I and
his contemporaries to issue cream-bodied
pottery wares molded as cauliflowers, pine-
apples, melons, and other organic forms.
Wedgwood's improved translucent green
and yellow glazes, introduced in 1759 and
1760, respectively, proved ideal for the
decoration of such pieces, which had previously been colored with mottled glazes.

GREEN-GLAZED WARE (1759 TO
c1800, AND REVIVED IN THE 1860S)

A translucent green glaze was perfected by
Josiah Wedgwood I during his partnership
with Thomas Whieldon and was used effectively from 1759 on molded cauliflower,
melon, and pineapple forms (*see* Fruit and
Vegetable Molded Ware) and on leaf-molded

dishes. By 1790 this glaze was being applied
to large ornamental pieces, sometimes with
contrasting enamel decoration. Foliate-
molded wares with an overall green glaze
continued to be manufactured by Wedgwood
during the 1860s as an addition to their
majolica range.

INLAID WARE
(FROM THE EARLY 1860S)

The laborious process of laying colored slip
into designs impressed into an unfired clay
body of a contrasting color was introduced
in Saint-Porchaire, France, in the 16th century.
This became known as Henri II ware. Rare
original examples of this technique were
keenly sought by 19th-century collectors and
a number of factories began to produce copies.
Walter Crane and Thomas Mellor designed
one of Wedgwood's most famous inlaid
exhibition pieces – a chess table complete with
chessmen, made for the 1871 London
Exhibition and eventually sold in New York

in 1898. Charles Toft, who joined Wedgwood in 1877, had been particularly associated with inlaid ware during his time at Minton but it was not made in any quantity at Etruria until the 1890s.

KENLOCK WARE (FROM c1901)

Introduced by Kennard Wedgwood at the beginning of the 20th century, Kenlock ware was decorated with brightly enameled patterns over a printed outline on either a black or red body.

(*See also* Lindsay Ware.)

LINDSAY WARE (FROM 1901)

Kennard Wedgwood was left in control at Etruria when his co-directors, Cecil and Francis Hamilton Wedgwood, were called away to fight in the Boer War. Kennard's enthusiasm for contemporary movements such as Art Nouveau led to the introduction of new designers and styles at the factory. Courtney Lindsay was commissioned to

design tiles and a new range of printed art wares. Lindsay ware was first issued in 1901 and displays distinctive Art Nouveau patterns incorporating stylized butterflies, peacocks, and other motifs from nature.

(*See also* Kenlock Ware.)

LUSTERWARE (FROM 1806)

The art of decorating earthenware pottery with a thin iridescent metallic film by the reduction of oxygen within the kiln atmosphere was developed in Mesopotamia in the 9th and 10th centuries and duly influenced both Islamic and European potters. Luster work is predominant on Hispano-Moresque tin-glazed wares (made by the Moorish invaders of Spain) and was used to great effect on Renaissance Italian maiolica. Luster decoration enjoyed a huge revival in the 19th century and formed a large portion of Wedgwood's output.

Thomas Bentley experimented successfully with luster techniques in London in the 1770s,

53

"Pineapple-molded teapot decorated with green and yellow glazes, *c*1760–65.

54

"Fairyland Lustre" vase decorated with the "Candlemas" pattern designed by Daisy Makeig-Jones, 1920s.

but there is no record of Wedgwood having actually produced lusterware until 1806 (although the unexplained mark "Josiah Wedgwood, Feby. 2d 1805" does appear on lustered pieces). Luster imitating solid metal-work, fired in an oxidizing atmosphere, was developed at about this time and Wedgwood's platinum-based "steel luster" and gold-based "copper luster" were among the first to be issued by the industrial potters.

Pink "splashed" luster (now referred to as Moonlight luster) was being made at Etruria by about 1810. The effect was produced by freely applying gold with a feather over Queen's ware and pearl ware. Variegated luster (produced by the marbling of gold, platinum, and iron lusters) was introduced a short time later. Commercial liquid lusters were developed in the mid-19th century and saw widespread use by 1900. In addition to painted, splashed and solid luster decoration, Wedgwood adopted the "resist" technique, in which a background pattern was painted over the glaze in a water-resistant medium before the article was dipped in a liquid luster; the "resist" subsequently burned off in the firing of the item.

William de Morgan, a Victorian potter who was closely associated with the Arts and Crafts Movement, rediscovered the process

SUSANNAH MARGARETTA ("DAISY") MAKEIG-JONES (1881–1945)

*Having persuaded Cecil Wedgwood to
employ her as a trainee painter in 1909,
Daisy Makeig-Jones was accepted on the staff
two years later and began to issue designs for
tableware. In 1913 she produced the first of
her Oriental dragon patterns, which were
probably inspired by James Hodgkiss's
experiments with powder colors: Her first
"ordinary" lustre designs, with dragons and
butterflies, were issued in 1914 and cleverly
combined gilt-printed outlines with lustered
powder-colored grounds. Having established
several successful ordinary lustre patterns of
fish, hummingbirds, fruit, and other subjects,
her more flamboyant "Fairyland luster"
designs were introduced in November 1915.
Makeig-Jones's "Fairyland lustre" was
produced by Wedgwood until 1931 and its
popularity established the firm's reputation as
a leading manufacturer of ornamental bone
china. The vivid colors and printed scenes of
imaginary figures in fantastic landscapes
proved immensely popular throughout the
1920s, until the Wall Street Crash
dramatically curtailed trade.*

*As eccentric in real life as the work she
produced, Daisy Makeig-Jones's behavior at
Etruria became increasingly unpredictable and
in April 1931 she was asked to retire and left
in a fury.*

JAMES HODGKISS (1867–1937)

*Active at Etruria from about 1900 to 1923,
Hodgkiss became chief designer in 1910 and
was involved in the development of the
powder colours and lustres associated with the
work of Daisy Makeig-Jones. He designed
many Oriental-style patterns, with gilt-printed
outlines over a powder-blue ground, and also
painted naturalistic scenes of birds in
landscapes on bone china dessert sets.*

55

**Pair of majolica
dolphin candlesticks,
c1870. Wedgwood
candlesticks of this
form also appear in
black basaltes and
Queen's ware. They
are believed to have
been originally
modeled by Josiah I.**

of smoke-reduced lusters and developed a new color range, including a distinctive ruby red. He and his partners originally decorated cream-colored earthenware "blanks" from outside sources, including Wedgwood. He is also known to have worked on Wedgwood black basaltes tiles.

MAJOLICA WARE (1860 TO c1940)

The trade name "majolica" was given to art pottery made in the second half of the 19th century that was decorated with translucent colored glazes. The term is derived from "maiolica" (early Italian Renaissance tin-glazed pottery), but the colored glaze technique itself was first established by a Frenchman, Bernard Palissy, in the third quarter of the 16th century, during his attempts to emulate Italian ware.

Ornamental majolica was first introduced by the Minton factory under the direction of Léon Arnoux, and soon rose to popularity at a time when original Palissy-type pottery was avidly being sought by collectors. Initially only a small proportion of Wedgwood's ornamental ware was decorated in this fashionable manner, but by the early 1870s the majolica range outstripped the production of all other decorative wares. Modeling standards in the Potteries were high at this time and the molded details perfectly complemented the massed colored glazes.

Wedgwood was commissioning designs from several independent artists and employing numerous apprentice painters from state art schools. However, output had greatly diminished by the beginning of the 20th century, partly due to changing tastes and

56

Splashed luster jug, cup and saucer, c1812. The splashed luster effect is now referred to as "Moonlight Luster".

57

Majolica stein with
hinged pewter cover,
*c*1870. The form is
taken from German
stoneware.

partly because of increasing government pressure to reduce the lead content of glazes for health reasons. Only very limited production of majolica continued at Etruria up until World War II. Today, examples of Wedgwood majolica are far less available than contemporary pieces by makers such as Minton and George Jones.

MAT GLAZES (FROM 1933)

An opaque egg-shell sheen can be achieved by the partial crystallization of a glaze during the post-fired cooling stage. Wedgwood's mat glazes, introduced in the 1930s, include "moonstone" white, blue, gray, straw, green, and "ravenstone" black (from 1958). Mat glazes were used extensively on the pure forms designed by Keith Murray and for the sculptural work of John Skeaping.

PEARL WARE (FROM 1779)

Wedgwood's "pearl white" body, introduced in 1779, seems to have developed from the "china glaze" earthenware that was being made by other Staffordshire potters from the mid-1770s. Pearl white was made superficially to look like porcelain by increasing the proportion of white clay and flint used in the existing creamware body, and by adding a slightly bluish tint to the clear glaze with cobalt oxide. One main advantage of the new creation was that not only could it be color-enameled over the glaze but, unlike creamware, it could also be decorated in underglaze blue in direct imitation of blue-and-white porcelain. Josiah I did not particularly care for his pearl white output but

> ### WILLIAM BEATTIE (FL 1829–64)
>
> Beattie's sculptural works were exhibited regularly at the Royal Academy from 1829. He moved to Stoke in about 1850 and worked as a figure modeler for several Staffordshire factories. Beattie joined Wedgwood in 1856, and his designs were issued in the Carrara statuary body and in majolica ware. Beattie returned to London in 1863, where he continued briefly as a freelance modeler for Wedgwood.

realized that it satisfied a competitive need. The name "pearl ware" is now used to describe such wares.

Underglaze blue printing on pearl ware arrived late at Wedgwood, a decade after Josiah I's death, but by the middle of the 19th century it had become firmly established (*see* Printed Wares). Wedgwood's "New Pearl ware" was introduced in 1809 and was used for George III's golden jubilee service (*see* Commemorative Wares).

PERSIAN AND RHODIAN WARES
(*c*1920 TO *c*1930)

Large decorative vases and plaques, boldly hand-painted with colorful Islamic patterns, were made at Etruria in the 1920s and were marketed as "Persian" and "Rhodian" ware. These designs are typical of the free-hand Arts and Crafts style that was introduced to Wedgwood by Alfred and Louise Powell.

(*See also* Millicent Jane Taplin.)

58

"Punch and Toby" majolica punch bowl, the handles modeled as the head of Mr Punch, the feet in the form of his dog Toby. Design registered in 1878.

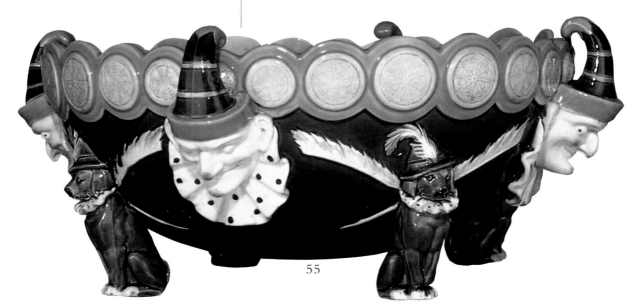

PORPHYRY WARE (FROM c1768)

By dusting the surface of creamware vases with metallic oxides, Josiah Wedgwood I was able to imitate hardstones such as porphyry, granite, and Blue John. Spectacular examples were made during the Wedgwood and Bentley partnership and became so popular that Josiah lightly referred to himself as "Vase Maker General to the Universe."

(*See also* Agate Ware.)

ROCKINGHAM WARE
(1865 TO 1940)

The brown-glazed earthenware developed in the last quarter of the 18th century by the Rockingham factory at Swinton, in Yorkshire, was widely emulated by the industrial potters. This soft, treacly glaze, tinted purplish-brown with manganese oxide, first decorated Wedgwood's creamware in 1865 and was generally left plain, or ornamented with acid-etched or wheel-engraved designs (*see also* Vigornian Ware).

TILES (c1765 TO c1800,
AND 1875 TO 1902)

Plain creamware wall tiles were produced by Josiah I in quantity for use in dairies, bathrooms, summer houses, and so on. Additionally, many such tiles were sent to Liverpool for printing by Sadler and Green, but there are few existing examples of these in comparison with their tin-glazed counterparts. Josiah I even produced jasper floor tiles for a short time, but these appear to have been too problematical and not cost-effective.

Soon after 1800 the manufacture of Wedgwood creamware tiles was discontinued but it was revived in the mid-1870s. At this time tiles were made in sets and were generally printed and hand-colored, but block printing was shortly introduced both for tiles and tableware (*see* Printed Wares). In 1880 George Anthony Marsden offered Wedgwood his patented process for decorating tiles. This mechanically imitated the "Barbotine" method of painting in raised slip, which was popular in France at that time. The production of "Marsden Patent Art Tiles" began at the end of 1881, notably with the stylized foliate designs of Lewis F Day. Marsden's

59

Selection of 19th-century under-glaze blue-printed pearl ware.

60

Porphyry ware vase, c1775. The Queen's ware body is surface-decorated to simulate porphyry stone (OPPOSITE).

process was also applied to a variety of art wares made between 1883 and 1888.

After much consideration, a separate tile department was set up at Etruria in 1882, and two years later a new series of tiles and plaques was introduced depicting classical subjects in bold relief. A slump in the tile trade in the late 1880s resulted in the closure of Marsden's decorating department, and in 1890 Wedgwood became a founder of the Tile Association, which attempted to stabilize the faltering industry by placing business mutually among its members. By the end of the century the fashion for pictorial and

A design by Helen J. A. Miles in watercolor depicting "September" for one of a set of calendar tiles.

art tiles had all but passed and in 1902 the tile department was finally closed down. Tile production was never considered to be more than a small contribution toward Wedgwood's business, and with its cessation the company was again able to concentrate fully on more viable areas of production.

TORTOISE-SHELL WARE (FROM c1754)

With the advent of liquid glazes and the double-firing process (*see* Cream-colored Earthenware), thin clay slips suspending colored metallic oxides could be painted or sponged on to a biscuit creamware body before glazing. On firing, the colors would flood into the clear glaze and form mottled "tortoise-shell" effects. This method of decoration was much used by the Wedgwood-Whieldon partnership and is often referred to

as Whieldon ware. However, this term is misleading as the same technique was employed by many of the partnership's contemporary rivals.

Josiah I's early experience of tortoise-shell ware led to the fine imitation hardstone vases made during the Wedgwood and Bentley partnership (*see* Porphyry Ware).

TREMBLAY WARE (FROM 1873)

In 1842 Baron du Tremblay patented the technique of decorating flatware that he had developed at the Roubelles porcelain works in France. This was known as *émail ombrant* and was derived from the lithophane process. Deeply graduated, central intaglio designs were flooded with a translucent glaze, usually green but occasionally gray or blue, and an almost photographic effect resulted that varied in tones of light and shade, depending

An earthenware bottle with underglaze oxide "tortoise-shell" decoration, *c*1775, and a similar bowl.

on the depth of the impression. In 1872 the Roubelles patent, along with the original molds and designs, came up for sale. These were acquired by Wedgwood, and Tremblay ware began to be made as an extension of the company's range of majolica production.

UTILITY WARE
(INTRODUCED 1942)

Due to the suspended production of patterned ware for the home market during World War II, Victor Skellern was called on to design plain white domestic "Utility" ware. The shapes were necessarily flexible and interchangeable: the cover of a vegetable dish could be reversed as a bowl; a sugar bowl and slop basin could double up as handleless cups; a teapot cover would also fit jugs as a lid.

VERONESE WARE (*c*1930 TO *c*1940)

The demand for expensive Wedgwood ornamental wares came to a fairly abrupt halt after the Wall Street Crash of 1929, threatening mass among the skilled work force at Etruria. In an effort to save jobs the Veronese range was quickly developed, combining simple contemporary forms with a variety of subtle glaze colors and sparse Art Deco-style silver luster decoration. The Veronese style formed a transition between the free-hand designs of the Powell school of decoration and the architectural modernism of Keith Murray.

VIGORNIAN WARE
(FROM *c*1876)

At the Paris Exposition of 1878, Wedgwood exhibited a sophisticated variety of mazarine

63

Pair of Victoria ware vases, decorated in neo-classical style, c1875. The creamware body is used here in an attempt to emulate the sumptuous ornamental porcelain wares of rival manufacturers.

blue and brown-glazed creamware under the trade name "Vigornian Ware". This was decorated by John Northwood's firm of Perkes & Co, in Stoke, with both naturalistic and formal acid-etched and wheel-engraved designs that exposed the pale body to a varying degree, depending on the depth of intrusion. This practice was first used on Wedgwood's 18th-century Chinese "Batavian" porcelain.

Porcelain

True "hard-paste" Chinese porcelain, made from high-fired China clay (kaolin) and China stone (fusible feldspathic rock), began to appear in Britain in the early 17th century. By the time of the Restoration, "china" collecting was a hobby enjoyed by the fashionable and wealthy. European hard-paste por-

celain was first produced in the early 18th century by the alchemist J F Böttger at the Meissen factory, near Dresden. "Soft-paste" artificial porcelain, in which the China stone is substituted by ground glass or frit (a calcined mixture of sand and fluxes) was first made in England in the mid-1740s. True English porcelain production was started in 1768 by William Cookworthy at Plymouth, using Cornish clay and stone. He transferred the factory to Bristol two years later under the management of Richard Champion, and in 1773 the latter bought both the factory and Cookworthy's patent (which conferred a monopoly over the Cornish ingredients).

When Champion applied to renew the patent in 1774 he met with stiff opposition from the Staffordshire potters, led by Josiah Wedgwood I, who demanded free access to Cornish materials. Champion compromised by limiting the patent's specification to cover only the quantity of ingredients used in respect to porcelain manufacture. Josiah had himself been experimenting with porcelain bodies and in a long letter to Bentley in 1776 gave his considered views on the technicalities and difficulties of its manufacture. Bentley urged him on several occasions not to infringe Champion's patent, but it seems that the sole reason Josiah I chose not to produce porcelain was his sound business sense – he had become the ceramic market leader and therefore saw no logical reason for diversification.

VICTORIA WARE

It used to be thought that "Victoria" ware consists of a Queen's ware body, but this is now generally thought not to be the case. It is probable that Victoria ware consists of

64

Bone china plate (from a service painted by John Cutts) and bone china teapot decorated with Dogs of Fo (the "Chinese Tigers" pattern), c1815. The pattern on the teapot was reintroduced in 1977.

glazed Parian (*see* Carrara Ware), although it may contain elements of creamware. It was manufactured in an attempt to emulate the sumptuous *pâte-sur-pâte* (*see* Carrara Ware) decorated wares of factories such as Minton, Coalport and Worcester. The method used was to place bas reliefs on colored grounds and then to glaze the item overall. The ware was ornamented with rich gilt relief work, modelled by Charles Toft or adapted from existing Jasperware designs.

BONE CHINA (1812 TO LATE 1820S, REINTRODUCED 1878)

The practice of strengthening a soft-paste porcelain body by the addition of bone ash originated at the Bow factory, London, in the late 1740s and was standardized at the Spode factory, Stoke-on-Trent, at the end of

65

Bone china plates designed by David Gentleman.

66

Bone china teapot from a service painted by John Cutts, c1815.

the 18th century. The manufacture of bone china was introduced at Etruria by Josiah Wedgwood II in 1812 after pressure from Josiah Byerley, the London manager, who was daily inundated with requests for "China tea ware."

Unfortunately, Josiah II lacked the marketing skills of his father and made two errors in the introduction of bone china: firstly, he enthusiastically sent Byerley casks of the new ware in June 1812, even though summer trade was traditionally slack; secondly, he did not hold back stock in order to build up a large promotional range. Even so, the new product found initial success in London. However, Regency taste demanded opulent designs and Wedgwood's patterns generally proved too restrained for fashionable buyers. Bone china production was soon scaled down and orders taken after 1822 seem to have been met from existing stock.

JOHN CUTTS (1772–1851)

Previously involved with the Pinxton porcelain factory in Derbyshire, Cutts began to work for Wedgwood in 1812 and most landscape decoration on bone china is now attributed to him. However, Josiah Wedgwood II expressed dissatisfaction with his painting and Cutts, seemingly in 1816, left to become an independent enameler at nearby Hanley.

67

Carrara ware bust of Venus, made in imitation of white marble, c1885.

The manufacture of bone china was revived at Etruria in 1878 by the three Wedgwood brothers, Godfrey, Clement Francis, and Lawrence, and has remained an important line until the present day.

(*See also* Wedgwood Tablewares.)

CARRARA WARE
(c1848 TO EARLY 1890S)

STATUARY The Art Union of London, formed in 1836, was instrumental in advancing the arts in Great Britain and its subscribers were entitled to partake in an annual lottery, which had contemporary works of art as prizes. Various other art unions gained much popularity when the movement was legalized in 1846, and lucrative premiums were paid to selected artists. However, contemporary marble sculpture was only affordable to the very wealthy and therefore statuary porcelain was added to the Art Union of London's 1846 prize list; thus the demand for Parian figures and busts was born, and it continued to grow.

Parian was a convincing imitation of white marble, and proved extremely successful for many manufacturers at the 1851 Great Exhibition. It is an unglazed porcellaneous material, similar in effect to Continental bisque porcelain, which shows slight translucency and has a fine texture. It was in fact the Minton factory that first used "Parian" as a trade name for its figures and busts in recognition of the fine white marble quarried at Mount St Elias on the Cycladic island of Paros. The term is now used generically to describe such examples from any factory, but Wedgwood actually marketed its own range as "Carrara statuary," named after the famous marble quarries at Carrara, in Tuscany, Italy.

Much of Wedgwood's existing sculptural range was reproduced in the Carrara body, but many additional models were specifically designed by contemporary artists, such as William Beattie, Albert Carrier de Belleuse, and Edward William Wyon. By using a "reducing machine" (effectively a three-dimensional pantograph, which was patented by Benjamin Cheverton and demonstrated at the 1851 Great Exhibition), exact copies of original sculptures could be reproduced on a different scale with relative ease. Once a suitably sized model had been made on the reducing machine, molds of the model were taken in plaster for the subsequent casting of porcelain. Large quantities of Carrara statuary continued to be produced at the Etruria factory until the early 1890s.

68

Pair of "Victoria" glazed Parian (Carrara) ware vases, or "barber bottles,", c1865.

69

Glazed Parian (Carrara) ware vase, heavily relief-decorated and colored to compete with the ornamental wares of Minton and Worcester, c1875 (OPPOSITE).

GLAZED ORNAMENTAL WARES (FROM 1861) In 1861 Wedgwood began experiments with colored glazes on the Carrara body and produced heavily ornamented and enameled Parian vases, from c1866 to c1880, in competition with those produced at the Minton and Worcester factories. (*See also* Victoria Ware.)

PÂTE-SUR-PÂTE (1888 TO 1889) The laborious technique of building up decorative images in layers of white porcelain slip on a contrasting ground was the specialty of Marc Louis Solon, who moved from the Sèvres factory, near Paris, to the Minton factory during the Franco-Prussian War of 1870. The demand for his work was so great that he

had to train several assistants, among whom were Charles Toft and Frederick Rhead, who both subsequently moved to Etruria. The latter made a limited number of *pâte-sur-pâte* decorated wares for Wedgwood using the Carrara body in 1888, but because of technical difficulties production was given up in the following year.

STONE CHINA (1820 TO 1861)

A dense, opaque, porcellaneous body, similar to Mason's Ironstone, was issued by Wedgwood in 1820 with underglaze blue prints and overglaze printed and enameled Oriental-inspired designs. It remained in limited production for 40 years.

Wedgwood Tablewares

70

**A selection of pieces
from a large Queen's
ware dinner and
dessert service, *c*1800.**

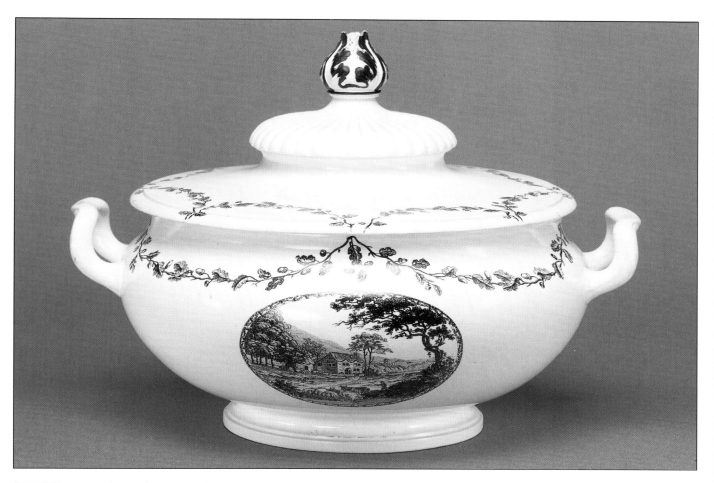

When Josiah Wedgwood I began production at the Ivy House works in 1759 he invited a cousin, Thomas Wedgwood, to become his journeyman. Seven years later he took him into partnership, with a one-eighth share of the profits in the sale of "useful" wares; this arrangement continued at Burslem and Etruria until the latter's death in 1788. As works manager, Thomas was responsible for overseeing both the quality and the physical manufacture of all "useful" wares. His contribution to the firm has always been overshadowed by the more glamorous associations of Wedgwood's "ornamental" wares, but without the careful control of utilitarian items there would have been little income available for indulging in the development of jasperware, black basaltes, and other wares.

As the partnership between Josiah Wedgwood and Thomas Bentley was confined solely to the production of "ornamental" wares, the introduction of tea ware in the black basaltes body led to a necessary reclar-

71

Queen's ware soup tureen, printed with a landscape after a wood engraving by Thomas Bewick, c1777. The "Bewick" pattern was reintroduced on Queen's ware in the 1950s.

72

Queen's ware "Nautilus" shape tureen and ladle, c1790. Josiah I was a keen amateur conchologist.

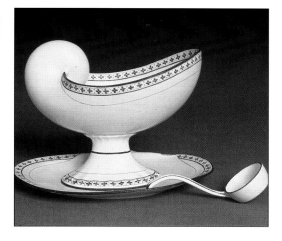

ification of the two separate arrangements. Replying to protestations from Bentley, Josiah defined useful wares as "vessels as are made use of at meals," no matter how richly decorated (as well as "Wash-hand basons [sic] and bottles or Ewers, Chamberpots, and a few such articles"). In doing this he provided the incentive for his cousin to continue improvements.

The "Husk" and "Frog" Services

Catherine the Great, Empress of Russia, was described by Josiah I as "a Woman of sense . . . fine taste and spirit." While being an important patron of the arts, she was equally known to others as "the devil at Petersburg," and Josiah's opinion was probably swayed by commercial interest. Catherine ordered two enormous Queen's ware services from him; the first, in 1770, was painted in pink with flower sprays within husk-festoon borders, for which it became known as the "Husk" service; the second, in 1773, was painted in "delicate black" with landscape views and is referred to as the "Frog" service. This was intended for use at the Chesmenski Palace, which was situated in an area known as La Grenouillère ("The Froggery") near St Petersburg, and each piece is suitably crested with a green frog.

Wedgwood's acceptance of the "Frog"

JAMES BAKEWELL (FL 1750–75)

Bakewell was active for Wedgwood at Burslem and at the Chelsea Decorating Studio (c1770–75), where he helped decorate pieces for the "Frog" service for Catherine the Great of Russia. He is known for his free-style flower painting on Queen's ware, both in purple and crimson monochrome and in black and yellow.

73

Queen's ware plate from the "Husk" service, made for Catherine the Great, Empress of Russia, 1770.

74

Queen's ware dessert plate from the "Frog" service, made for Catherine the Great, Empress of Russia, 1773-74. The scene depicts Castle Acre, Norfolk.

service commission was risky, as any war or political upheaval in Russia could have resulted in the account not being settled. In addition, the sheer volume of work involved distracted from the normal output of the

75

Detail of a crest from the "Frog" service.

Chelsea Decorating Studio: it seems that as many as 33 people devoted their time to this service at Chelsea. The scenes were to depict "real Views of Great Britain" and Josiah even contemplated the idea of having them all specially commissioned. In the end they were principally taken from paintings and prints, although a Cheshire artist, Stringer, was employed to draw a number of local views around Staffordshire.

The service was completed in 1774, at a cost to Catherine of £2,290 12s 4d, and was displayed in London before being shipped to its final destination. A handful of similarly decorated polychrome pieces (without the crest) have survived. These were once thought to be "trials" that had proven too expensive for full production in comparison to monochrome painting. However, it is more likely that they were manufactured in the second half of 1774 for public display. In 1788 Josiah Wedgwood proudly remembered the Russian commission as "the most superb service I ever sent to the Continent."

Crested and Armorial Services

The fashion of personalizing a ceramic service with its owner's coat of arms developed from armorial engravings on metalwork and was popularized by way of the enameled Chinese export porcelain services commissioned and imported by the European gentry. Crested and armorial Queen's ware services became an essential part of Josiah I's business, as witnessed by the "crest books" preserved at the Wedgwood Museum. Initially such items would be hand-painted at Etruria, but this was found to be uncompetitive: Guy Green (*see* John Sadler and Guy Green) could charge his customers as little as one-sixth of Wedgwood's production cost by arranging the transfer printing and hand-enameling of armorial bearings. Modern coats of arms are usually reproduced at Etruria by lithographic transfer printing.

Victorian Tableware

By the mid-19th century most of the decorated tableware made at Etruria was transfer printed. Underglaze blue printing had been introduced there in 1805 and the blue-printing department was managed by Abner, son of Thomas Wedgwood, until his death in 1835. A few of the first patterns, such as "Ferrara" and "Landscape,", have remained in production to the present day. The botanical "Water Lily" or so-called "Darwin" service pattern (such a service is known to have been in the

76

Representative pieces from the "Gordon Highlanders" service, painted with various regimental devices within thistle borders. The service was commissioned by the Marquis of Huntley for the 12th Regiment of the Gordon Highlanders in 1809.

77

Queen's ware plate, printed and painted with the arms of Honeywood and Courtenay, c1796 (OPPOSITE).

possession of the descendents of Charles Darwin) was introduced in 1808.

From the 1860s, printed patterns fell into two classes – "common" and "best." "Common" patterns were used on plain shapes, utilizing a body that was midway between cream-colored and pearl ware, and include "Filigree," "Broseley," "Botanical," and "Willow." "Best" patterns were reserved for more ornate shapes, using a pearl ware body dipped in a pearl glaze, and include "Water Nymph," "Dahlia," and "Clarendon."

The Japanese influence became evident from 1862, and the combination of open border patterns and rich decoration led to a wider use of printed wares. One of the most successful border patterns was designed by Christopher Dresser and was shown at the 1867 Paris Exhibition. The influence of Emile

Lessore's French genre style led to the expansion of the decorative dessert ware range. Many of the newly introduced patterns were colored in by hand over printed outlines, giving a hand-painted appearance.

The important London retailers, such as Thomas Goode and Mortlocks, played a significant part in the design and development of dessert wares during this period. Some even had their own studios for the purpose of both designing and hand-painting. Such design work would be supplied to the manufacturers for reproduction, and ready-painted pieces would generally be sent for firing.

In 1870 Wedgwood was commissioned by Mortlocks to reproduce its early cream-colored earthenware. Once mastered this was used for a variety of purposes, and the "Hans Sloane" botanical style of painting –

78

Underglaze blue-printed pearl ware "Water Lily" pattern mug and jug. The service is sometimes referred to as the "Darwin Service" because a service of this pattern was in the possession of the descendants of the famous English naturalist Charles Darwin.

79

Two "Spanish"-shape plates, painted by Emile Lessore, 1871 (BELOW).

popular on Chelsea porcelain of the 1750s – appeared in a printed and painted form. Several new dinner and dessert ware shapes were brought out at this time; some were adapted for use in the majolica, and other earthenware, ranges. In his position as art director, Thomas Allen oversaw the introduction of a series of contemporary figure patterns, such as "Ivanhoe," "Playmate," and "Banquet" (shown at the 1878 Paris Exhibition).

Minton's patented ovens were installed throughout the Etruria works and as a result

bone china was reintroduced in 1878. Consequently the Wedgwood tea ware range was greatly expanded and exclusive patterns began to be designed for the bone china body. Inspired by the success of Royal Worcester porcelain, Wedgwood released lavishly molded and richly gilded and "jeweled" hand-painted wares, worked on by a number of artists such as Fred Dudley, T Hall, and W Hartshorne. Thus by the end of the 19th century the tableware range had widened to cater to a large variety of tastes.

80

Underglaze blue-printed pearl ware "Hibiscus" pattern plate, *c*1810.

20th-century Designer Services

Decoration must be designed for the shape, and must add something relevant to it . . . . there is no such thing as "Traditional" or "Contemporary" design. These are merely convenient labels. Design is either good or bad: if good, it lasts; if bad, it doesn't.

(*VICTOR SKELLERN – WEDGWOOD'S ART DIRECTOR, 1934-65.*)

Traditional tableware regained control at Etruria in the early 20th century due to much necessary rationalization (*see* John Goodwin). Up until the 1930s Alfred and Louise Powell produced many refreshingly simple flower and foliage designs, as well as charming prints such as "Rural England." Useful wares coming from Millicent Taplin's hand-painting studio (*see* Millicent Jane Taplin)

81

Representative pieces from a "Moonlight Luster" shell-molded dessert service, *c*1810–20.

continued the "craft" style, and even Daisy Makeig-Jones's early designs for useful wares showed restraint. Makeig-Jones produced a series of nursery ware patterns, like "Thumbelina," "Brownies," and "Noah's Ark," as well as her "Celtic Ornaments" patterns, which were derived from motifs shown in the 6th-century *Book of Kells*.

The arrival of Victor Skellern in 1934 firmly established a new era in the history of Wedgwood's functional tableware production, with free use of external, as well as factory, designers. Skellern was personally responsible for Wedgwood's first lithographic transfer-printed tableware pattern, "Charnwood" (introduced in 1944). Among his many other printed designs are "Forest Folk," "Meadow," "Greyfriars," and "Evenlode." His work was founded on the sound philosophy quoted above. It is therefore not surprising that he was chosen to design Wedgwood's wartime utility ware.

VICTOR GEORGE SKELLERN (1909–66)

As art director, John Goodwin's safe, traditional approach helped Wedgwood to survive difficult times. In the 1930s a renewed spirit of modernism emerged at Etruria, culminating in the decision to build a new factory. In 1934 Victor Skellern took over from Goodwin and for 31 years devoted himself to developing harmonious modern utilitarian forms.

Skellern had previously worked under Goodwin at Etruria, while also training at the Burslem and Hanley Schools of Art. He left Wedgwood in 1930 to study at the Royal College of Art but returned four years later as replacement art director. In his new position he introduced many freelance artists to the company as well as designing in his own right. He also worked closely with established Wedgwood designers and took great interest in the application of advanced technology, especially the controversial introduction of lithographic printing (see Processes of Manufacture).

Wedgwood promoted its contemporary functional designs at several exhibitions in the 1930s; Skellern's reputation was firmly established at the Grafton Galleries in 1936, where the public could "select and criticise from the economic as well as the aesthetic point of view" (price lists were available). Before retiring in 1965, Skellern travelled widely in Europe and North America.

82

Windsor gray plate printed with the "Travel" pattern designed by Eric Ravilious in 1938. Although this pattern was designed before World War II, it was not introduced until c1953.

ERIC WILLIAM RAVILIOUS (1903–42)

After training at the Eastbourne School of Art, Eric Ravilious won a scholarship to the Royal College of Art, where he studied under Paul Nash. He first exhibited watercolors in 1926 and shortly afterward began to undertake mural commissions. In 1933 he took part in a tableware design scheme organized in the Potteries. The results were exhibited at Harrods a year later and he consequently received a number of industrial design commissions.

Ravilious worked for Wedgwood fairly steadily between 1936 and 1940. His first commemorative design to be issued was the mug for the coronation of King George VI in 1937 (see Commemorative Wares), and he went on to produce many successful tableware patterns (see Dinner Services). However, due to the restrictions imposed by the outbreak of World War II, several of his designs were not issued in quantity until the 1950s.

In 1940 Ravilious was appointed an official war artist. Two years later, his plane went missing while on patrol.

83

Printed designs by Eric Ravilious: "Alphabet" pattern mug, designed 1937; "Persephone" pattern plate, designed c1938; George VI Coronation mug, originally designed for Edward VIII in 1937.

84

Representative pieces from an extensive Queen's ware dinner and dessert service, c1810.

A modern approach was also taken by Keith Murray, whose spare tableware patterns, such as "Lotus," "Iris," and "Green-Tree," perfectly complement the pure forms they decorate. Murray's last major design for Wedgwood, the "Commonwealth" service (*see* Keith Murray) could indeed stand on its own, without surface decoration.

Wedgwood tableware made for London's Berkeley Hotel in *c*1932 bears a highly stylized red and green "B" monogram. The Savoy Hotel approached Wedgwood just before World War II for a large quantity of wares (nearly 13,000 pieces), but due to hostilities these were not actually put into full production until 1954. Designed by Lady Robertson, wife of the architect Sir Howard Robertson, the Savoy "Royal Barge" pattern (depicting a traditional Royal Thames Barge) is still in use today.

Eric Ravilious's 1930s tableware patterns include "Persephone" (1936), "Afternoon Tea" (1937), "Travel" (*c*1937) and "Garden" (*c*1939), but many of these were not produced in quantity until the 1950s due to the outbreak of World War II. One of Richard Guyatt's best-known commissions was for Liberty of London in 1953 – a jug and beaker lemonade set printed with views of old London churches, known as the "Oranges and Lemons" pattern.

Relieving ten years of utility ware, the ceramics industry in the 1950s produced many colorful contemporary designs that led to the stylized geometric patterns of the 1960s, such as Wedgwood's "Yellow Diamond." In the 1960s and 1970s Wedgwood's "oven-to-table" ware was strongly influenced by Studio pottery: "Blue Pacific" and "Sterling" are such examples. Pastel colors dominated the 1980s (Wedgwood's "Pastel Strata," for instance), while recent black "designer" wares complete a cycle by echoing the black basaltes first produced over 220 years ago.

Special Editions and Commemorative Wares

85

One of a pair of jasper medallions made to commemorate the Storming of the Bastille on July 14, 1789. Josiah Wedgwood I rejoiced at the fall of this symbol of the corrupt Bourbon monarchy and ensured that relevantly titled "Bastille Medallions" were rushed into production.

Alongside the production of "useful" wares, Wedgwood has always undertaken special orders, and issued limited editions and commemorative lines.

Limited Editions

Josiah I's most famous "ornamental" achievement was the reproduction in jasperware of the Portland Vase. Once thought to have been fashioned from semiprecious stone, this important Greco-Roman cased-glass vase, dating from the first century AD, is housed at the British Museum and has recently undergone extensive re-restoration. In 1845 it was deliberately shattered with a piece of sculpture while on view. The early history of the vase is obscure, but it is known to have been in the Palazzo Barberini in Rome, and was acquired by the Dowager Duchess of Portland

86

20th-century Royal-Blue jasperware copy of the Portland Vase, issued in a limited edition of 50 (LEFT).

87

First edition white on black jasperware copy from the original edition of the Portland Vase, 1790. Note the translucency of the bas-relief work, particularly evident on the tree foliage (BELOW).

WILLIAM HACKWOOD (C1757–1839)

On September 20, 1769, Josiah Wedgwood informed his partner, Thomas Bentley, that he had "hired an ingenious Boy last night for Etruria as a Modeller." The ingenious boy was William Hackwood, who became Wedgwood's chief ornamental modeler until 1832. Little of Hackwood's work was original but he proved invaluable in adapting and finishing the busts, reliefs, and designs purchased by Wedgwood in London. A testament to his ability is the fact that he worked with Josiah I on the first edition of the Portland Vase. Hackwood retired after a staggering 63 years of service with Wedgwood.

HENRY WEBBER (1754–1826)

The son of a Swiss sculptor, Abraham Webber, Henry Webber was taken on by Wedgwood in 1782 and was recommended by Sir Joshua Reynolds as "the most promising pupil in the Royal Academy." In 1787 he was sent to Rome to join John Flaxman, Jr, and on return translated his studies of antique reliefs into usable models. Webber worked on the first edition of the Portland Vase and also designed the "Sydney Cove" medallion (see Commemorative Wares). Henry Webber remained with Wedgwood until about 1795.

in 1784 from the renowned collector of classical vases, Sir William Hamilton.

After the Duchess's death it was purchased at auction in 1786 by her son, the third Duke of Portland. Within days Josiah Wedgwood had borrowed it to commence a series of trials to produce faithful replicas. The exact number of the vases made at that time was probably around 30, of which fewer than 20 are known to remain in existence. Wedgwood has since issued several editions of the Portland Vase (*see* John Northwood), including

the 1839 version in which the naked figures were draped in response to Victorian modesty!

"RESTRICTIVE PRACTICES"

Several wealthy connoisseurs subscribed to the original Portland Vase issue, effectively making it the first pottery "limited edition." However, the concept of limited lines was not really known in Josiah I's time – he would naturally try to make as much as he could hope to sell. Therefore, one should not rely on the number of survivors of any particular issue as a definitive gauge of the quantity produced, unless supported by further evidence. This rule particularly applies to easily discarded items such as medallions. Only a handful of the original "Sydney Cove" medallions (made with clay sent from Sydney Cove, Australia, in 1779) is known, whereas it is likely that hundreds were produced.

In time, a principle of deliberately confining the output of certain ceramic lines developed alongside any necessary self-restriction. One of Wedgwood's ultimate limited lines, other than complete one-of-a-kinds, was the "Unique" ware produced by Norman Wilson, often at weekends, which intriguingly combined traditional bodies and experimental finishes (*see* Norman Wilson).

In 1930 Wedgwood held an international competition to design a vase commemorating the bicentennial of Josiah I's birth. Among the many applicants were John Skeaping and his then wife, Barbara Hep-

JOHN NORTHWOOD (1837–1902)

Northwood owned the Stoke-on-Trent glass engraving firm of Perkes & Co and, as a glass master in his own right, produced the first known copy of the Portland Vase to be made by exactly the same techniques as the cased-glass original. In 1877 he was engaged by Wedgwood to finish the reliefs on a limited edition of 15 jasperware Portland Vases, using lapidary polishing methods. His company also decorated a quantity of Wedgwood's mazarine blue and Rockingham glazed wares (see Vigornian Ware).

worth, but the contest was won by a Danish glass designer, Emmanuel Tjerne. A limited number (about 16) of the vases were produced for presentation to the judges and Tjerne.

Children's mugs showing the reversible heads of Cinderella and the Fairy Godmother after a Rex Whistler design, were produced in very small quantities in around 1955. The same applies to sets of Laurence Whistler's "Outlines of Grandeur" Queen's ware plates, issued at about the same time, but this was mainly due to marketing difficulties. Eduardo Paolozzi's silk-screen plates (*see* Printing) of 1970 were deliberately restricted to 200 sets.

In 1976 Glenys Barton became artist in residence at Barlaston, and her sculptural work was exhibited in London a year later. Most pieces were produced in limited editions of four copies, although a few ranged between 10 and 50.

88

Jasperware "Sydney Cove Medallion," designed by Henry Webber and modeled by William Hackwood, with figures of Hope attended by Peace, Art and Labor, in 1789. The small jasper body (only 2 in/5 cm in diameter) contained a portion of clay found at Sydney Cove, Australia, and sent to Josiah Wedgwood through Sir Joseph Banks.

Wedgwood's 1978 "Egyptian Collection" comprised figures, plates, and plaques derived from Tutankhamun's treasure and other sources. The editions ranged from 250 (for sphinxes and gilded basaltes plaques) to 3,000 (for the miniature "Beloved of the Great Enchantress" plaques).

The two World Wars directly influenced two of Wedgwood's most important 20th-century limited editions – "Liberty" ware and "Old London Views.". These were released in the United States and Canada to help War Relief funds. "Liberty" ware was the brainchild of Mrs Robert Coleman Taylor of New York, who placed an order through the retailer William Plummer & Co in 1917. The range was sold entirely on subscription from Mrs Taylor's own home, and all orders received before Armistice Day were honored before the copper printing plates were deliberately destroyed. She managed to sell 9,251 pieces of "Liberty" ware and her efforts raised the sum of $14,203.

The first American edition of "Old London Views" was limited to 10,000 sets and printed on the back were "First Edition 1941." A Canadian edition of 5,000 sets was issued in the same year, bearing an appropriate backstamp.

Commemorative Wares

ROYAL COMMEMORATIVES

As can be seen in the Royals Gallery of the Wedgwood Museum at Barlaston, the company has always maintained close connections with royalty. Both the Etruria and Barlaston factories have been visited by members of the Royal Family and specific events have been commemorated by special designs.

Josiah I was allowed to style himself "Potter to Her Majesty" after pleasing Queen Charlotte (consort of George III) with a creamware service. Later he celebrated the king's "return to health" in 1789 by issuing a series of specially designed jasperware medallions. The golden jubilee of George III's accession to the throne was celebrated on 25 October 1809, and the factory produced some

89

Bulb pot made to the commemorate Golden Jubilee of King George III. This was celebrated on October 25, 1809, when the King entered the fiftieth year of his reign.

RICHARD GERALD TALBOT GUYATT (1914–)

Guyatt's association with Wedgwood began when he designed the company's stand for the British Industries Fair. Shortly afterward he was appointed consultant designer from 1952 to 1955, a post that he again held from 1967 to 1970. His first design for Wedgwood to be produced on a large scale was the award-winning mug issued in 1953 to commemorate the coronation of Queen Elizabeth II. At this time he also designed a jug and beaker set to retail at Liberty of London, which subsequently inspired his "Oranges and Lemons" pattern (see Wedgwood Tablewares). Guyatt's later work for Wedgwood includes a number of commemorative wares.

---

atypically bright and florid commemorative pearl ware in response to public complaints that nothing new was coming from Etruria.

Pieces produced for the silver jubilee of King George V and Queen Mary in 1935 heralded the beginning of Wedgwood's large-scale production of royal commemorative wares. Dame Laura Knight designed a bone china loving cup and cover in 1936, at the request of Victor Skellern, for the impending coronation of Edward VIII. Eric Ravilious engraved a mug design for the same occasion. These were not issued due to the future monarch's abdication, but Ravilious's design was adapted for the coronations of George VI (1937) and Elizabeth II (1953).

In 1937 Professor Sigismund Kisfalud De Strobl exhibited a marble bust of Princess Elizabeth at the Royal Academy and a copy was commissioned by Wedgwood to commemorate George VI's coronation. The moonstone glaze version was limited to 27

copies, whereas the black basaltes issue was originally far larger and was repeated for the 1959 Wedgwood bicentennial and the 1977 silver jubilee of Elizabeth II.

Wedgwood's solid "Windsor grey" body was perfected in 1952 and used for a large quantity of portrait-molded ware commemorating Elizabeth II's coronation in the following year. Queen's ware with lavender reliefs designed by Arnold Machin was also released at this time, as were mugs designed by Richard Guyatt. (Guyatt also produced mugs for the Investiture of the Prince of Wales [1969], the Royal Silver Wedding [1973] and the Silver Jubilee [1977].) Later, in 1971 and 1979, Machin designed portrait medallions of Queen Elizabeth and the Duke of Edinburgh.

90

Commemorative mugs printed with designs by Richard Guyatt: American Bicentennial, 1976; Silver Jubilee, 1977; Royal Silver Wedding, 1974; Coronation of Elizabeth II, 1953; Prince of Wales Investiture, 1969.

The marriage of Princess Anne to Captain Mark Phillips in 1973 was marked with a Queen's ware mug by Richard Guyatt, together with thousands of blue jasperware portrait medallions. Prince Charles's wedding to Lady Diana Spencer in 1981 was commemorated by an array of limited editions: 500 black basaltes busts by David McFall; 100 fully titled blue jasperware vases; 50 smaller vases with profile portraits; 3,000 blue jasper medallions of the prince by Arnold Machin, and 2,000 similar medallions of the princess (by Michael Dillon). Prince William's birth in 1982 was recorded on the "Peter Rabbit" nursery ware design, which was first introduced in 1949.

AMERICAN INTEREST WARES

American history has been widely depicted on Wedgwood wares ever since Josiah I established trade links with the New World. As detailed in the first chapter, he was sympathetic to the colonists' cause and issued various medallions depicting American and French revolutionaries.

To commemorate the American Bicentennial of 1976, Wedgwood issued a number of limited-edition jasperware pieces: pairs of plates with the American eagle and portraits of the 13 signatories of the Declaration of Independence (5,000); five-color plates with George Washington portraits (300); goblets

---

MRS PATIENCE LOVELL WRIGHT (1715–86)

Born in Bordentown, New Jersey, Mrs Wright came to London in 1772 as a painter and modeler in wax. Her portrait of Benjamin Franklin was reproduced by Wedgwood in jasperware and black basaltes in about 1775, as was an engraving by her son of George Washington, in 1789.

CLARE VERONICA HOPE LEIGHTON (1900–)

Clare Leighton was born with a natural artistic talent and her studies at art schools in both Brighton and London led to a fascination with wood engraving. A selection of her work was published in 1930 and she subsequently wrote and illustrated a number of books. In 1939 she moved to America, becoming a US citizen six years later, and in 1950 she was commissioned by Wedgwood to produce a series of woodcuts to illustrate New England industries (see Commemorative Wares). These were issued as underglaze charcoal sepia prints on 12 rimless "Coupe" shaped plates that were specially designed for the series by Leighton in conjunction with Victor Skellern.

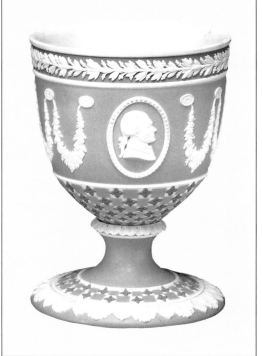

91

Pearl ware commemorative plate, underglaze-printed with a scene of the United States Naval Academy in 1838. Commissioned by Jones, McDuffee and Stratton in 1958 (ABOVE).

92

Jasper-dip goblet ornamented with portrait medallions of Washington and Jefferson, made for the American Bicentennial in 1976 (LEFT).

HERBERT W PALLISER

In 1940 Wedgwood commissioned Palliser, a teacher of sculpture at the Royal College of Art, to model a series of birds based on Audubon's Birds of America for the retailer W H Plummer and Co of New York. These were cast in bone china and enameled by Arthur Holland.

93

Jasperware plate from the "American Independence" series, issued in 1976 to commemorate the American Bicentennial. The scene depicts "Paul Revere's Ride."

ALAN PRICE (1926–)

Price joined Wedgwood in 1953 after studying at the Royal College of Art. A year later he began working as a designer attached to the New York office, where he subsequently concentrated on wares with an American theme (see Commemorative Wares).

with George Washington and Thomas Jefferson portraits (200); and mugs featuring the American eagle (500). The latter was designed by Richard Guyatt, as was a Queen's ware mug (5,000) of the same subject.

The 1976 "American Independence" series of six blue-and-white jasperware plates included scenes such as the "Boston Tea Party" and "Victory at Yorktown." A few years later the "America's Heritage" series of plates was issued in a limited edition of 15,000 sets with molded inscriptions and bas-relief scenes such as "The West by Land" and "The Heartland by Rail." The Peace and Posterity Jug, which was commissioned by the Wedgwood Collectors Society, is taken from a

creamware jug dating from about 1800 and shows the population statistics of the various states of the Union.

Other Wedgwood American interest wares included a paperweight commemorating the famous Liberty Bell, which was cast in London in 1751, damaged in transit, and recast in Philadelphia before being hung. The jasperware campanological piece is inscribed "Proclaim Liberty throughout all the Land." The "Presidents" plate, showing the 37 presidents up to Gerald Ford, was designed by the American artist Karen Worth and issued in an edition of 3,000. Arnold Machin modeled a bust of Franklin Delano Roosevelt, produced in both Queen's ware and Windsor

94

Queen's ware plate from the "New England Industries" series, designed by Clare Leighton in 1952. This woodcut print depicts "Ice Cutting."

gray, as well as a jasperware portrait medallion of the same subject.

Alan Price's "Federal Cities" series includes the "Boston" bowl, the "Washington Presidential" bowl and the "St Lawrence Seaway" plate. A 1951 issue of 12 photolithographic printed plates depicts the "New England Industries," after woodcut designs produced by Clare Leighton, with a variety of scenes such as "Whaling," "Tobacco Growing," and "Logging."

In 1881 Wedgwood produced the first "calendar" tile for the Boston ceramics retailing firm of Jones, McDuffee and Stratton. These were printed with historical and topographical American views and were given away to regular customers each Christmas. The tradition continued until 1929, by which time the Wedgwood tile department had closed, causing the printing to be done at Etruria on blanks from local Staffordshire

95

Queen's ware bowl printed after a design by Alan Price in 1959 and commemorating the signing of the Articles of Federation at Philadelphia on July 9, 1778.

tile companies. These were issued in varying quantities but the 1910 "Mayflower Arriving" tile, made for the retailer's centenary year, is known to have had an order of 12,000 copies.

Jones, McDuffee and Stratton were Wedgwood's US representatives for printed commemorative ware, and from the 35 "Wedgwood Old Blue Historical Plates" registered in 1899 grew more than 1,000 such designs by the time of the firms' dissociation in the 1950s. These pieces form an interesting and unique historical series.

Wedgwood's US version of the traditional English toby jug appears in the guise of Elihu Yale, benefactor of Yale University. This jug was modeled by Prof Robert G Eberhard of the Department of Sculpture at Yale, and produced for the Yale Publishing Company in 1933. The likeness is based on a portrait of Yale painted in 1717 by Enoch Zeeman.

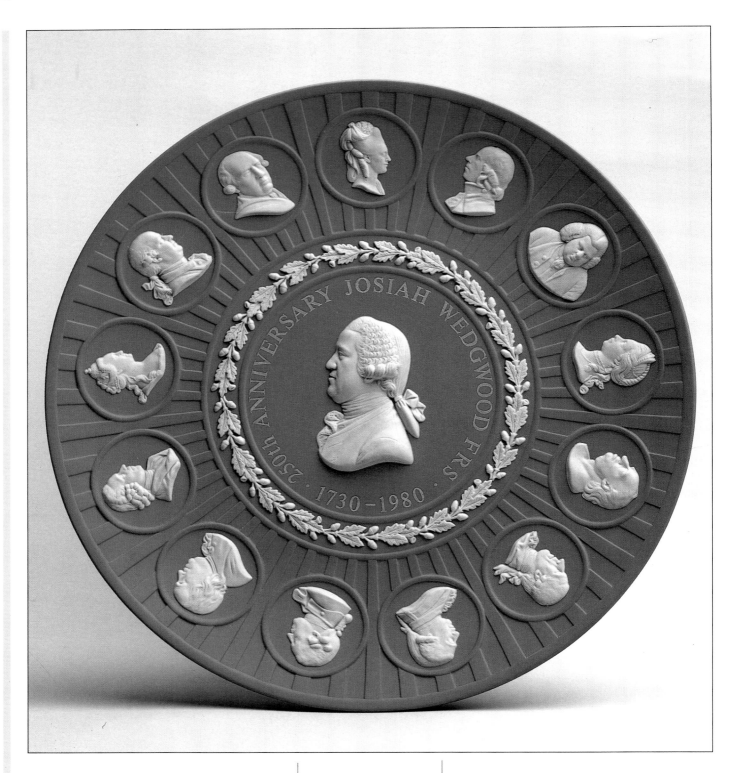

"JOSIAWARENESS"

In defiance of the financial chaos resulting from the 1929 Wall Street Crash, Wedgwood staged spectacular celebrations for the bi-centennial of Josiah I's birth in 1930. Not surprisingly, this event prompted several commemorative issues.

John Goodwin designed a blue jasper-dip "Apollo" vase, with a relevant Latin inscription, which was made in a limited edition of 50 (the first was presented to Queen Mary). A black basaltes portrait bust of Josiah was released in a controlled amount. This was re-modeled by E A Austin (fl 1904–47) after

96

Jasperware "Josiah Wedgwood and his Circle" plate commemorating the 250th anniversary of Josiah I's birth, issued 1980. The central portrait of Josiah, modeled by Joachim Smith in 1773, is surrounded by such contemporaries as his wife, Sarah, his partner, Thomas Bentley, and one of his patrons, Catherine the Great of Russia (OPPOSITE).

97

The first Wedgwood jasperware Christmas Plate, 1969, showing Windsor Castle, England, and the first Christmas mug, 1971, showing Piccadilly Circus, London.

Charles Toft, who had previously taken it from John Flaxman's original bust on Josiah's tomb. A large selection of Queen's ware was also issued, printed with portraits of the founder of the Wedgwood company after the 1782 painting by Sir Joshua Reynolds.

The 1930 bicentennial also occasioned 50 replicas of the encaustic "First Day's Vases," painted with suitably adapted texts (*see* The Wedgwood and Bentley Partnership in chapter one). Twenty years later, to mark the closure of the Etruria works after 181 years of operation, six "Last Day's Vases" were produced. Eric Ravilious's last design for Wedgwood was for the "Barlaston" mug, made in 1940 to commemorate the opening of the new factory.

20TH-CENTURY DESIGNER COMMEMORATIVES

A public interest in the remembrance of great people, places, and events was recognized early in Wedgwood's history and has been fully exploited in the 20th century.

Eric Ravilious is mentioned earlier in respect to his royal commemoratives, but one of his own personal favorite designs was for the 1938 annual Thames boat race between crews from Oxford and Cambridge universities. A Queen's ware vase and bowl show three successive stages of the race, and the bowl interior has a scene of the Piccadilly Square festivities on Boat Race Night. Richard Guyatt's prize-winning Elizabeth II "Coronation" mug is previously noted but he also won an award from the Council of Industrial Design for his 1968 black and white jasperware "British Sporting Centres" mug, which was released in a limited edition of 500.

As well as his patriotic mug and royal portrait medallions, Arnold Machin modeled a bust of Sir Winston Churchill. This, like his F D Roosevelt bust, was issued both in a Windsor gray and Queen's ware body. Norman Makinson designed the 1951 "Festival of Britain" mug, which depicts the famous South Bank "Skylon" monument and the Festival symbol.

Victor Skellern was responsible for the "London" jug made for Liberty of London in 1959 for the 250th anniversary of Dr

Samuel Johnson's birth. This Queen's ware piece is printed with William Wordsworth's poem, "On Westminster Bridge," and Johnson's famous line, "When a man is tired of London, he is tired of Life." Skellern also designed the 1961 "Gilbert and Sullivan 50th Anniversary" mug.

Designers from outside the company were commissioned for the "British Castles" series of bone china plates and the 1976 "Menai Suspension Bridge 150th Anniversary" plate. David Gentleman was responsible for the "British Castles" edition, with the first two views, Harlech Castle and Woburn Abbey, being issued in 1977. A Welsh designer, Islwyn Williams, was suitably chosen to honor Thomas Telford's link across the Menai Strait (from the Isle of Anglesey to the Welsh mainland), and this plate bears a dual-language backstamp.

The 400th anniversary of William Shakespeare's birth was honored in 1964 by the Queen's ware "Shakespeare" mug (printed with 12 characters from his plays), a reissued black basaltes portrait bust and medallion, and a green jasper plate depicting his birth-

98

The "London Jug" designed by Victor Skellern and produced for Liberty of London in 1959.

99

Two bone china plates from the "Castles and Country Houses" series, designed by David Gentleman. These are the first two views, issued in 1977, and show Woburn Abbey, England, and Harlech Castle, Wales (RIGHT).

SIR HUMPHRY DAVY

place. Other famous Englishmen commemorated by Wedgwood in the 20th century include Charles Darwin (a "Water Lily" pattern mug commissioned by the Wedgwood Collectors Society); Sir Humphrey Davy (1978 bicentennial mug); and General James Wolfe (1959 bicentennial jug).

The Royal Observatory at Greenwich was founded in 1675, and to mark its tercentennial Wedgwood produced a limited-edition bone china plate printed with portraits of the first

100

Queen's ware mug commemorating the bicentennial of the birth of the English scientist Sir Humphrey Davy, issued in 1978. Davy worked with Josiah I's son, Thomas, on early photographic experiments.

11 Astronomers-Royal, together with star-gazing devices. Six years earlier, Apollo Eleven made a successful moon landing and Wedgwood's "Man on the Moon" plate serves testimony to this event.

However, one of Wedgwood's most popular series since 1969 has been the jasper-ware "Christmas" plate, which not only appeals to collectors but also provides a perfect solution to the annual problem of "What shall we give to Auntie"!

Processes
of Manufacture

101

**Black basaltes self- framed plaque of
Zeno, founder of the Stoic school of
philosophy, with encaustic painted
ground, c1775.**

Josiah Wedgwood I, a leading figure of the Industrial Revolution, was instrumental in transforming a traditionally local trade into an international operation. Until the time he decided to set up his own empire, most Staffordshire potteries were small operations that returned a moderate income. Indeed, Josiah's legacy from his father, due to be paid when he reached the age of 20, was only £20. However, by 1795, he had amassed an estate worth then around £½ million. Such financial success was secured by a careful balance of artistic achievement and mass-production methods.

Creating Form

THROWING

One of the most fundamental potting techniques is that of hand "throwing" a ball of pliable clay centered on a revolving horizontal wheel. The use of "jiggers" and "jolleys" (revolving disc-molds) in conjunction with a "profile" (a stationary tool) allows numerous identical shapes to be formed repeatedly on the wheel. Plates may be made in quantity by sandwiching a bat of clay between a revolving jigger and a stationary profile. Equally, cups can be formed by much the same method, using a jolley and profile.

TURNING

Larger ornamental pieces may be shaved on a horizontal lathe, while in a "leather-hard" (partially dry) state, using stationary cutting tools. Josiah I made improvements to existing pottery-turning lathe technology and used such machinery extensively.

Engine-turning lathes employ an eccentric motion, which allows repetitive patterns to

When a thrown piece has dried to a consistency known as "cheese" or "leather" hard, it is ready to be turned on a lathe. Surplus clay is shaved off with great precision.

Many shapes are best made by casting. Slip (liquid clay) is poured into a plaster of Paris mold. A coating of clay forms on the inside of the mold, and the excess slip is poured away.

Bas-relief ornaments are applied by hand to jasperware using a technique that has not altered since the days of Josiah I.

be cut with the aid of a guide tool. Josiah I saw such a machine at work in Birmingham in 1763 (*see* Matthew Boulton), and installed his own at Burslem in the same year. Carving pottery by use of an engine-turning lathe continues to be a highly skilled operation.

MOLDING AND CASTING

The disadvantage of throwing and turning is that only articles of circular section may be made in this fashion. The use of plaster of Paris for mold-making (seemingly introduced into Staffordshire in around 1745) opened up endless possibilities for ceramic designers.

PRESS-MOLDING A basic method of ceramic relief ornamentation is to press clay into a plaster of Paris, or fired clay, female "pitcher" mold. The molds absorb a little moisture from the clay, thus allowing easy removal, and the resulting image is attached on to the intended vessel by moistening the back or using creamy clay "slip" as an adhesive. This is the technique employed for Wedgwood's bas-relief decorated wares.

Due to the evaporation of its water content, clay shrinks when fired by approximately 2 to 20 per cent, depending on the size and composition of the item. By continually molding and firing "male" clay reliefs, in ever decreasing sizes, it is possible to obtain finely detailed, reduced versions of large models. Wedgwood's early bas-relief work was produced by this method.

SLIP-CASTING Press-molding has been greatly replaced by the slip-casting technique, in which semi-liquid clay is poured into a plaster of Paris mold. A layer of slip adheres to the interior surface and, when sufficiently thick-

ened, any surplus is poured away. As the cast dries it shrinks from the mold, which can then be opened and then reassembled for further use.

ASSEMBLING On removal from molds, articles generally require "fettling" and often need "repairing." A fettler finishes a molded piece by trimming off any seams and mold-marks. The presence of such marks on pottery and porcelain suggests poor quality control and the use of worn molds. A repairer is a skilled workman who assembles figures and other ornamental wares from a number of casts using adhesive slip and, in the case of intricate work such as figures, assembles additional supports to prevent sagging of the piece in the kiln.

Surface Decoration

GLAZING

A glaze is essentially a thin coating of molten glass which makes a porous body impermeable as well as enhancing its appearance. As

102

Majolica jardinière modeled by Hugues Protat and painted by Emile Lessore, _c_1870.

103
Cane ware pot-pourri vase
painted with Oriental
flowers in *"famille rose"* style
enamels, *c*1815–20.

viously stated, opaque tin oxide glazes were not part of Wedgwood's output. The opaque finish of the matt glazes introduced by Norman Wilson in 1933 is actually achieved by partial crystallization (*see* Matt Glazes).

Transparent and translucent glazes give benefit to the underlying body colour and originally contained powdered lead ore (*see* Cream-colored Earthenware). Safer, leadless glazes came into production around the turn of this century, mainly as the result of a government health enquiry in 1898.

PAINTING

Painted patterns can be executed either before or after glazing, or a combination of the two. The underglaze palette is necessarily limited and, up until the mid-19th century, was restricted to blue (obtained from cobalt oxide) and brownish-purple (from manganese oxide). An exception to these is the extremely rare underglaze red seen on early Chinese porcelain. In contrast, overglaze enamels have an extensive palette, but do not have the protection of a glassy coating and may require several firings.

Josiah I developed a range of matt "encaustic" colors in order to imitate the red figure decoration of early Greco-Italian pottery. This Athenian style was introduced in around 530 BC and reversed the earlier black

104

Black basaltes cream jug, cup and saucer with encaustic painted "Running Anthemion" border. c1775.

Designs for tableware are printed from hand-engraved patterns and then enriched by hand painting in ceramic colors.

figure wares. The ancient method of representing red figures on a black ground entailed painting the background black in order for the reddish clay body to show through where required. Wedgwood's technique (which he patented in 1769) was to paint the figures and details in "encaustic" colors on a black basaltes body.

GILDING

The application of gilt detail was avoided as much as possible by Josiah I, who initially experienced many technical difficulties. The most common method of gilding in the 18th

105

Rosso antico and cane ware potpourri vases and pierced covers, painted with Oriental flowers in *famille rose*-style enamels, *c*1815–20.

century was to grind gold leaf with honey, painting with the resulting paste as required. A further low temperature firing was necessary to allow the gold to harden, followed by burnishing to brighten the resulting dull effect. Honey gilding is easily worn away in the course of time.

Durable mercuric gilding was introduced at the Derby porcelain factory by John Hancock, Sr, and soon spread into general use. (Hancock also worked for Wedgwood from 1816.) The new method incorporated five parts mercury to six parts gold in a finely ground mixture to which fluxes were added. The mercury passes off when fired, and the

remaining dull gold detail is then burnished to a high shine after firing. The introduction of "steel" and "silver" luster is also credited to Hancock (*see* Lusterware).

SLIP DECORATION

By coating a clay body with a contrasting slip, which is then partially carved away, various *sgraffito* designs can be obtained. Notable exponents of this technique at Wedgwood were Harry Barnard, Millicent Taplin, and Norman Wilson. Slip can also be trailed in the manner of cake icing, a method used by Barnard and others, and employed for "impasto" work – a similar effect to heavily brushed oil paint. Marbled surface slips can give the effect of semiprecious hardstones (*see* Agate Ware).

PRINTING

All free-hand decoration is by nature time-consuming and costly; hence the popular use of printing methods, either individually or in conjunction with hand work. Printed designs on ceramics can be either under the glaze (sometimes with the addition of onglaze painting and gilding) or over the glaze (often with added enamel colors). Underglaze prints enjoy the same protection as underglaze painting, while overglaze prints run the risk of abrasion.

TRANSFER PRINTING Most of Josiah I's transfer printing was done in Liverpool from 1761 to 1793 (*see* John Sadler and Guy Green), although in 1765 he bought the right to undertake his own printing and exercised it by at least 1786. Sadler and Green's transfer printing was onglaze but the same method can also be used underglaze.

The first stage in producing a transfer print is the skilled engraving of a copper plate

106

Black basaltes figure of a Sphinx with gilt details, late 19th century.

107

Queen's ware teapot and hot water jug, showing traces of gilding in the molding, most of which has been worn away, *c*1765–70.

with the required design. A warm mixture of oil and powdered coloring oxide is then applied to the plate and the excess wiped off.

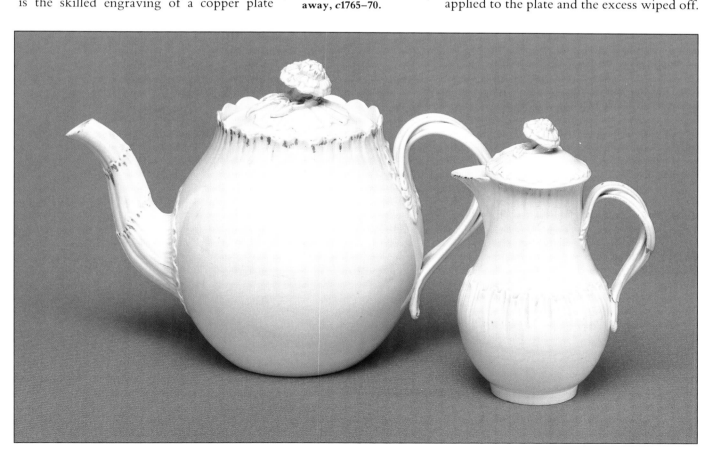

Next, a sheet of wet tissue paper, backed by a flannel pad, is sandwiched between the prepared plate and a press or roller. When peeled off, the paper is carefully laid on the required unfired ceramic surface and rubbed on the back. The previously reversed image is thus transferred positively to the porous surface and the backing paper is gently washed away.

Underglaze blue transfer printing was introduced at Etruria in 1805 as a result of the successes of rival firms. "Flowing" or "flow" blue became popular in the mid-1830s and was still being made in the 1870s. This involved the deliberate addition of a volatilizing agent into the kiln atmosphere, causing the printed images to blur into the glaze.

BAT PRINTING A method of transferring a softer printed image was employed toward the end of the 18th century: this substituted the tissue paper with "bats" of soft glue or gelatin. Warm oil was applied to a stipple-engraved copper plate and the impression was lifted on to the surface of a bat that was then dusted with powdered pigment. The color adhered to the pattern and was then introduced to a suitable surface.

This process was the forerunner of Wedgwood's modern printing method, whereby an automatic transfer machine takes an imprint from a prepared copper plate via a gelatin pad and then lowers it on to the intended article.

108

Queen's ware rococo coffee pot, overglaze-printed with "Liverpool Birds" by Guy Green, *c*1775.

109

A selection of Liverpool overglaze printing on Wedgwood Queen's ware, *c*1770–80 (OPPOSITE).

LITHOGRAPHY Wedgwood first used lithographic transfer printing in 1863, a method now widely employed by ceramic decorators. Taking a greasy crayon, a design can be laid on to a suitable surface that is then moistened and "inked." Ceramic pigment is attracted to the grease but repelled by the water; thus reversed impressions can be taken on special paper and then transferred positively to the required object. At first, such designs were drawn on limestone tablets; these were superseded by metal drums, used as rollers; and today rubber provides a vastly improved support.

Polychrome lithographic printing was developed as a relatively inexpensive way of imitating the semi-hand craft method of enameling over transfer-printed outlines. It also accepts a wider range of gradation and tone than do older methods.

PHOTOLITHOGRAPHY In 1854 a French porcelain manufacturer, Lafon de Canarsac, invented a photographic technique for ceramic decoration. He displayed his work at the 1862 London Exhibition and earned himself a gold medal. During the ensuing decade the technique of overglaze photographic image printing was developed.

In 1876 a photographer was installed at Etruria and a series of monochrome drawings taken from Old Masters and the French school was reproduced on pottery using the photographic method. Colonel Crealock (*see* Henry Hope Crealock) had already undertaken some animal painting for Wedgwood

HENRY HOPE CREALOCK (1831–91)

A professional soldier, Crealock served in many parts of the world, including the Crimea, India, China, and South Africa, before retiring having reached the rank of lieutenant-general in 1884. As an artist and writer he recorded events related to his military career as well as animal and sporting subjects. Through his friendship with Clement Francis Wedgwood some of Crealock's work was reproduced at Etruria from 1874 to 1877 by the photolithographic printing process (see Processes of Manufacture).

when, in 1876, he negotiated the reproduction of a series of his stag drawings by photolithography.

The technique did not achieve great popularity: a letter from Godfrey Wedgwood (a partner at Etruria from 1859 to 1891) reveals that photographic wares were not intended "for the millions" but for "the landlords who appreciate really artistic things."

SILK-SCREEN PRINTING The modern silk-screen process, in which pigment is dispersed through a fine mesh blocked with a predetermined design, was used to dramatic effect for a set of limited-edition plates in 1970 (*see* Eduardo Luigi Paolozzi). From 1960 onward it has been used to great benefit in the printing of gilt detail.

110

Queen's ware "Parapet" teapot, printed and painted with the "Agricultural Implements" pattern, *c*1805 (BELOW RIGHT).

111

Underglaze blue-printed pearl ware "Landscape" pattern *bourdalou, c*1830. Wedgwood referred to these chamber pots for women as "coach pots" (BELOW).

112

Bone china "Fairyland Luster" plaque decorated with the "Elves in a Pine Tree" pattern designed by Daisy Makeig-Jones, 1920s.

POWDER GROUNDS In the 18th-century English porcelain factories drew heavily on Oriental influences and naturally imitated Chinese "powder-blue" grounds. Originally such grounds were produced by blowing powdered pigment through a screen over a surface with oiled detail, the dust adhering only to the intended design. A quicker way of producing the same effect is by the use of a compressed air spray, known as aerography. Wedgwood used this method extensively, especially on bone china in the 1950s.

An alternative technique for simulating a powder ground involves laying down a solid color and then stippling it with a sponge.

(*See also* Daisy Makeig-Jones.)

Kilns and Kiln Furniture

Josiah Wedgwood I was elected a Fellow of the Royal Society in 1783 and soon after gave papers on his kiln thermometer, or "pyrometer." Before the invention of this gadget, the only way a kiln master could judge temperature was to observe the color of the fire within by removing a small plug set in the wall. Josiah's pyrometer relied on measuring, with graduated rulers, the shrinkage encountered in the kiln by variously composed set-sized clay cylinders. "Buller's" rings were a development of this method, and "Seger" and "Orton" cones later provided an alternative measure. The temperature within modern commercial kilns is controlled by thermo-couples, which adjust the fuel supply.

113

Extracts from Wedgwood's first pattern book, probably started c1700, showing enlargements of Queen's ware border patterns, c1775-80.

Brick-built, bottle-shaped kilns were employed from Josiah I's early days and remained in use throughout the history of Etruria. These were necessarily packed when cold and emptied when cool enough, after coal firing. To avoid any damage from direct contact with flames, the unfired objects were packed into fireclay boxes, or "saggars," which were sealed to avoid the entry of unwanted gases. In salt-glaze production the saggars were pierced to assist in the formation of sodium alumina sulphate (*see* White Salt-glazed Stoneware).

Modern commercial kilns allow wares to be stacked on fire-proof trolleys that move very slowly through a long tunnel in which the temperature increases toward the center and falls toward the exit. Wedgwood's first gas-fired china "glost" (glaze-firing) tunnel

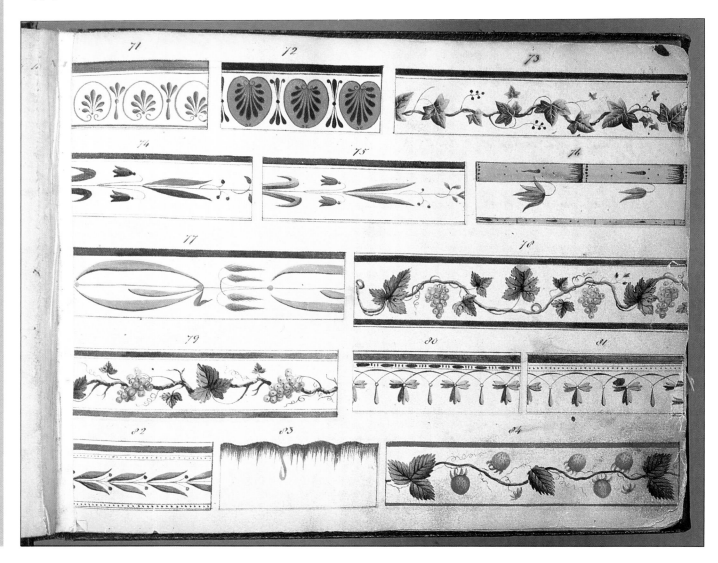

114

Queen's ware table centrepiece (epergne) as illustrated in Wedgwood's 1774 Catalogue.

oven and electric "muffle" (enamel-firing) kiln were installed under the guidance of Norman Wilson at Etruria in 1927. In 1930 the Wedgwood/Wilson oil-fueled glost tunnel oven was developed, and from the following year it was used for all earthenware and china glazing.

Electrically heated Swiss-made Brown-Boveri double-tunnel ovens, capable of biscuit and glaze firings, were installed at the modern Barlaston factory in 1940. These were the first to be seen in the Potteries. They maximized valuable stacking space by removing the need for saggars.

Collecting and Identifying Wedgwood

Wedgwood jasperware
medallions are found
incorporated into
various objects, such as
clock cases and furniture.

What Shall I Collect?

In actual fact, this frequently asked question can often mean "What shall I collect that is going to prove a sound investment?" This is a dangerous approach toward collecting anything because, as in any market, prices can fluctuate on supply and demand. Wiser questions to ask oneself are, "Do I like it?", "Can I afford it?" and "Is it genuine?" Many dedicated collectors are driven by a seemingly unstoppable accumulative instinct and readily overcome the first two questions. Through the constant handling of their own prized possessions, and through committed research, they can also gain an ability to answer the third question.

Collecting Wedgwood

Neo-classical Wedgwood appeals to collectors worldwide, especially in the United States, where many large displays of "Federal" wares have been put together in the 20th century. Writers generally focus on 18th- and early 19th-century Wedgwood because, historically, this is the most innovative. However, as more and more early pieces are absorbed into private and museum collections, the whole aspect of acquiring good examples of old Wedgwood constantly remains under review and new directions bear consideration.

A surge in the price of "Fairyland luster" was recently experienced, while at the same time there has been obvious relaxing in the area of traditional wares. The major auction houses held regular sales of early Wedgwood in the 1970s but today only a trickle of good examples appears in their catalogs. It takes a brave individual to instigate the sale of a large collection of like objects during a slack period, but this will often rekindle interest among existing collectors and attract a new group of enthusiasts.

Buying at auction can be time-consuming and is not without its pitfalls, but at least the

116

Queen's ware teapot, enameled with flowers, *c*1770. The visible damage could be rectified by modern restoration. In buying a damaged piece, a collector can decide how much, if any, camouflage work to undertake.

117

Black basaltes hedgehog bulb pot, a model that has remained in production from the 18th century to the present day. The body is packed with moss or soil before being planted with bulbs.

118

Victorian jasper-dip jug based on the Portland Vase. Note the added drapery on the male figures, in response to the modesty of the period (OPPOSITE).

larger sale rooms now offer some guarantee of authenticity. However, it remains for the individual to decide whether or not to exceed the printed estimate and, if so, by how much. In this respect it may be prudent to seek advice from a reputable specialist. Any fee incurred for professional assistance can ultimately help secure a genuine lot at a realistic price, thus avoiding any future embarrassment or worthless "investment."

For those who would rather buy at a pre-determined price, there are alternative methods of securing Wedgwood wares. Most antiques dealers now clearly mark their goods and, short of a bit of haggling, a buyer knows precisely what a given piece is going to cost. An advantage of Wedgwood's continuing two-fold output of both traditional and modern lines is that brand-new examples, many superficially identical to earlier products, can be purchased from a network of international retail outlets. Callers at the Wedgwood Visitor's Centre's shop, at Barlaston, may easily be tempted to come away with anything from an ashtray to a complete dinner service!

Any hand-worked artifact is likely to prove expensive, so before embarking on the formation of a Wedgwood collection it is important to establish a realistic budget. A price guide to items illustrated in this book is toward the rear of the book.

Identifying Wedgwood

By definition, it is impossible to build an old house; by the same reasoning, one cannot re-create a genuine antique. However, it is possible to manufacture readily passable copies of early Staffordshire pottery, and some caution should be exercised when purchasing old Wedgwood.

MISLEADING MARKS

Voyez told our Evidence yesterday that he did not regard any action for putting Wedgwood & Bentley upon his seals . . . . He meant another W & another B, & not his Prosecutors. Besides he knew from a late Trial of the same nature which he saw between two Sheffield Manufacturers for the same thing, that we could not hurt him. For though it was proved that one had put the others mark upon his goods the Jury only brought in one shilling damages.

(JOSIAH WEDGWOOD I WRITING TO THOMAS BENTLEY, 13 FEBRUARY 1776.)

The above statement makes it clear that un-scrupulous potters were producing and selling contemporary copies of Wedgwood & Bentley seals, although some were less daring in their piracy – as witnessed by black stoneware intaglios impressed "WADGWOJD" in minute lettering.

The impressed mark "VEDGWOOD" appears on English earthenware plates apparently made by William Smith & Co of the Stafford Pottery, Stockton-on-Tees, Yorkshire, which seems to have occasionally sought to pass off its wares as true Wedgwood. Another misleading mark found on earthen-wares is "J. WEDG WOOD" (with a slight space or dot between the "G" and the second "W"). These were made by John Wedge Wood, a distant relative of Josiah Wedgwood, in the middle of the 19th century.

A "WEDGWOOD & CO." mark was legitimately used by Ralph Wedgwood, eldest son of Josiah I's cousin and partner, Thomas Wedgwood, who set up a pottery in

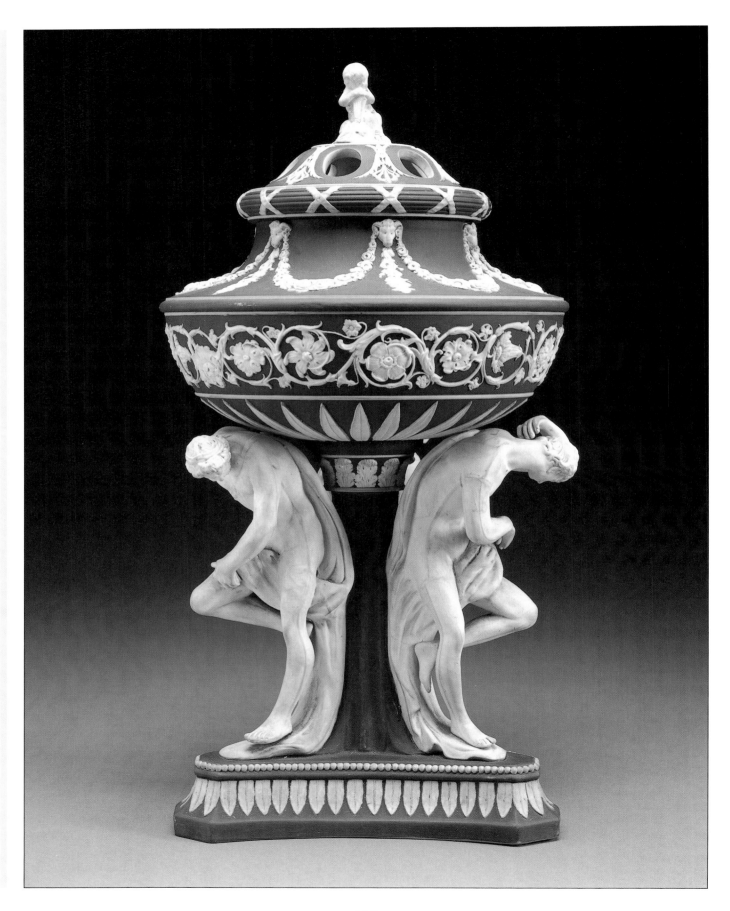

119

Black basaltes "Michelangelo Lamp," the covered bowl having three burners, c1785–90. This form combines a copy of a Hellenistic bronze bowl with supporters derived from a silver-gilt crucifix by Antonio Gentile de Faenza (1531–1609). It is stated that Gentile's figures were cast from models by Michelangelo.

120

Jasperware vase in the form of a "Michelangelo Lamp," 19th century. The mold seams on the limbs of the supporting figures have not been "felted" as painstakingly as they would have been on an 18th-century example. (OPPOSITE).

Burslem before moving to Ferrybridge, in Yorkshire. A similar mark occurs on wares produced by Podmore, Walker and Co (Podmore, Walker & Enoch Wedgwood), which subsequently became Wedgwood & Co but whose products are unconnected with Josiah Wedgwood & Sons Ltd.

To add to the puzzle, it is possible that Ralph Wedgwood produced the 18th-century enameled creamware and pearl ware figures bearing impressed "WEDGWOOD" marks. These are thought to have been farmed out by Josiah I, but the names of the potters Enoch, John, and Ralph Wood have also been forwarded as likely candidates.

It is important to remember that Wedgwood lines have been imitated contempor-

aneously throughout the firm's history and the inclusion of an apparently bona fide mark does not always guarantee a genuine article. For example, a recent sudden rise in auction prices for "Fairyland luster" led to the appearance of luster pieces made by other factories in the 1920s with no deceptive intent, bearing spurious Wedgwood marks that had replaced any previously ground-off markings. This sort of deception is fairly easily spotted, but the situation is further complicated if the mark itself is genuine. For technical reasons ornamental Wedgwood vases were bolted on to their bases from 1771, so it is not impossible to remove the bolt and replace a possibly damaged vase with either a cleaner example, a later example, or even a vase that has been

111

manufactured in an entirely different factory!

A list of marks appropriate to the wares discussed and illustrated in this book is given in the following section.

MISLEADING STYLES Alongside the handful of 18th-century rogue potters who dishonestly imitated Wedgwood, there were many Staffordshire manufacturers who simply wanted to climb on the bandwagon, including John Turner of Lane End, William Adams of Burslem, and Humphrey Palmer and James Neale of Hanley. Although much of their work was copyist, one should not be too dismissive as, technically, their wares can often hold their own against contemporary Wedgwood pieces.

Recently made Continental Wedgwood-style jasperwares are unlikely to fool the majority of collectors: they are normally molded with the background and relief work in one piece, and the ground color is later applied around the raised image. However, some early German and French factories came close to the quality associated with Wedgwood, although on close inspection there are many stylistic and manufacturing differences.

Queen's ware has been imitated by various English and European factories but, in truth, Continental *"faïence fine," "steingut," "flintsporslin,"* or whatever, bears little resemblance to the English creamware body and often fails in its overambitious nature. Replacements for the "Husk" service (*see* Wedgwood Tablewares)

were made in Russia in the early 19th century by a factory at Morje, near St Petersburg, run sequentially by Freidrichs, Poskotchine, and Emelyanov. These come fairly close to the original when seen in isolation.

Experiencing Wedgwood Wares

There are many aspects of Wedgwood potting techniques that cannot be properly explored without close inspection. Those readers fortunate enough to enjoy easy access to study collections have a distinct advantage over those who must contend with looking at "pots behind glass." It is frustrating not to be able to handle objects whose original function was indeed to be handled; so how does a budding collector begin to gain confidence in purchasing Wedgwood?

Despite spiraling overheads, many dealers are perfectly happy for their customers to touch goods on display. Auction houses are generally committed to opening their cabinets to any prospective bidder, which is probably the least intimidating way of setting about handling Wedgwood of some age. Overall quality is a fundamental consideration in dating a piece of Wedgwood, and it is far wiser to begin viewing an object from this angle and then work backward toward any confirming mark, rather than vice versa.

121

Jasper-dip plaque of the "Dancing Hours," modeled by John Flaxman, Jr, c1778. This is Wedgwood's best known bas-relief subject and has remained popular until the present day. Note the well-defined quality of the relief work on this early example. (BELOW).

122

Jasper-dip vase
decorated with the
"Dancing Hours" bas-
relief frieze, 19th
century.

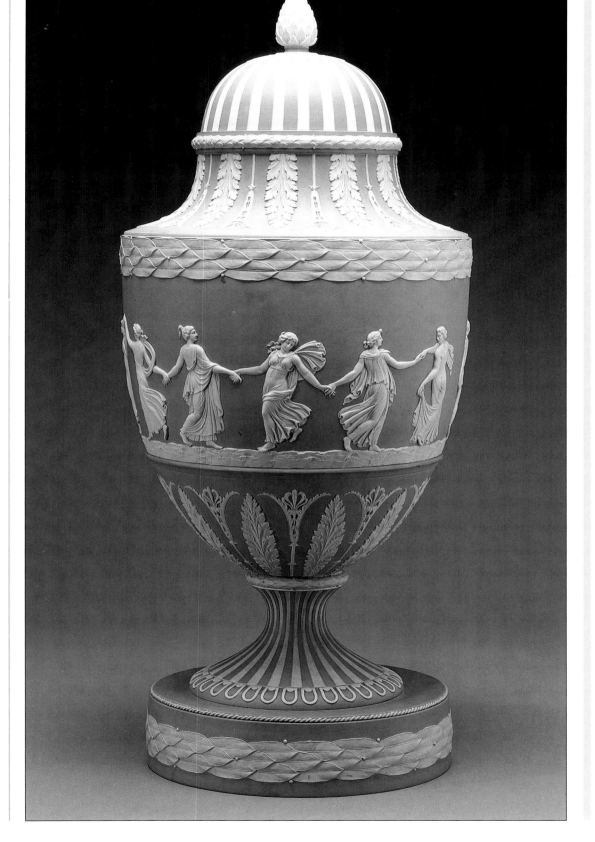

"Dragon" and "Butterfly" luster vases with designs by Daisy Makeig-Jones, *c*1915 (LEFT AND RIGHT). Such "Ordinary Lustre" designs should not be confused with the distinct "Fairyland Lustre" range.

ORNAMENTAL WARES

Early Wedgwood jasperwares display a smooth and uniformly grained body bearing sharp and well-defined bas-relief work. Often this was laboriously undercut to heighten the contrast between the background and ornament. Later examples have rather chalky reliefs and a generally coarser touch. Of course, it is possible to "re-finish" stoneware with wet and dry paper, both in an attempt to remove scratches from old examples and to smooth the surface of later ones.

Perhaps the ultimate way of experiencing an old piece of Wedgwood jasper is to handle a first edition Portland Vase – nothing quite compares afterward. Some later Portland Vases incorporate identifying marks, such as "JN" and " " incised on the 1877 "Northwood" edition and the initials "TL" incised on the Thomas Lovatt version of about 1880. As previously mentioned, the 1839 version also has added drapery (*see* Limited Editions).

The basic principal of jasperware identification can be extended to other dry bodies such as cane ware, *rosso antico,* and black basaltes. However, there is an added problem with the latter: the fashion for polishing such pieces with black shoe polish to give a satin-like patina can also disguise (maybe not intentionally) any restoration work that may have previously taken place.

USEFUL WARES

It is extremely difficult to attribute any early "tortoise-shell" or "agate" ware to a given manufacturer without positive archaeological evidence. This is equally true of white salt-glazed stoneware and "common" unglazed red ware, although there is reason to believe that impressed pseudo-Chinese seal marks incorporating the letter "W" were used at Wedgwood's Brick House works.

To a certain extent, the yardstick that early creamware is a fairly deep cream color, and that later 18th-century creamware is paler and more evenly and thinly glazed, is correct. Wedgwood's Queen's ware should certainly be light to the touch and show some signs of genuine wear. Artificial "aging" of day-to-day wares, by using abrasive paper, stones, or files, is fairly easily detected as the wear tends to be regular and flowing in a limited

direction. In normal use such pieces would generally experience abrasion to "high spots" and a varying degree of overall wear to any surfaces that come into contact with cutlery.

Early creamware and pearl ware tend to display "crazing" – a series of fine surface cracks on the glaze, caused by uneven post-firing cooling between body and glaze. However, a similar effect can be innocently caused by heating such wares if they are placed in a domestic oven.

Appendices

Marks

Josiah Wedgwood I was the first Staffordshire potter to make a point of fully marking his wares – selling them by reputation as well as physical appearance. It is likely that marks began to be impressed as soon as he set up on his own account in 1759. The practice certainly seems more common in the mid-1760s, and from 1769 virtually all products bear the Wedgwood trade name. In contrast to the importance placed on his own reputation, Josiah I would not permit any of his artists to sign work – William Hackwood tried to bend this rule and was reprimanded!

WEDGWOOD

Generally considered to be the first impressed marks used, 1759–69.

WEDGWOOD

The standard impressed mark from 1780 onwards (useful wares only, 1769–80). Printed on bone china in various colours, c1812–22. Printed in underglaze blue on blue printed wares.

The earliest Wedgwood & Bentley partnership mark, impressed, c1769.

WEDGWOOD
& BENTLEY
Wedgwood
& Bentley

Impressed on ornamental wares, 1769–80.

Impressed or embossed on a circular applied pad of clay. Found underneath the plinths of black basaltes vases and on the pedestals of busts and figures, 1769–80.

Impressed underneath the plinths of black basaltes, "hardstone" and "Etruscan" vases, centred around the bolt hole, 1771–80.

W. & B.

Wedgwood
& Bentley

Impressed on small seals and cameos, normally with an appropriate catalogue number, 1769–80.

Rare impressed mark. Found only on chocolate-brown and white seals, usually formed of two jasper layers and with polished edges, 1769–80.

Wedgwood.

Impressed, c1780-95 and probably for a time after Josiah I's death.

WEDGWOOD & SONS

Very rare impressed mark. Used for a short period in 1790.

WEDGWOOD'S STONE CHINA

Printed on stone china, c1820–61.

WEDGWOOD ETRURIA

Impressed, c1840–45.

PEARL
P

Impressed on pearl body, c1840–68.
Impressed on pearl body, 1868 onwards.

WEDGWOOD

The Portland Vase mark. Printed on bone china (and rarely on Queen's ware), 1878–1900.

WEDGWOOD

Later version of the Portland Vase mark, with three stars beneath, c1900 onwards. The words "BONE CHINA" added from about 1920 onwards.

WEDGWOOD
ETRURIA. ENGLAND

Rare impressed mark. Found on some Queen's ware, c1891–1900.

ENGLAND

Additional impressed or printed mark, added to comply with the American Customs Regulation, known as the "McKinley Tariff Act", introduced in 1891.

MADE IN ENGLAND

Additional impressed or printed mark from about 1898, but not used invariably until about 1908.

WEDGWOOD

Impressed sans serif type mark, used from 1929 onwards. The old type continued to be used on some specimens after this date.

WEDGWOOD
Bone China
MADE IN ENGLAND

Modern bone china mark. First introduced in 1962.

Modern Queen's ware mark. Introduced in about 1940.

N W
or
NORMAN WILSON

Additional impressed or painted marks on Norman Wilson "Unique" ware.

ENGRAVED BY WEDGWOOD STUDIO

With engraved patterns from 1952.

Wedgwood ® is a registered trademark of Wedgwood Limited of Barlaston, Stoke-on-Trent, Staffordshire. Marks reproduced by kind permission of Wedgwood.

Date Codes

In 1860 a system of impressed date codes was introduced on Wedgwood earthenwares. From 1860 to 1906 the last letter of a three-letter mark denotes the year of manufacture.

★★O = 1860	★★A = 1872	★★A = 1898
through to	through to	through to
★★Z = 1871	★★Z = 1897	★★I = 1906

From 1907, the number 3 replaces the first letter (originally a month code), and from 1924 the number 4 replaces the number 3.

3★J = 1907	4★A = 1924
through to	through to
3★Z = 1923	4★F = 1929

From 1930 the actual year was impressed, first as the last two numbers of a code, eg ★★30 = 1930, and later as just two figures, eg 53 = 1953.

The other letters incorporated into Wedgwood date codes indicate months and potters, but these were often misplaced and can be confusing. Also, these impressed marks are not always entirely legible.

Addresses

Collectors Clubs

Wedgwood Collectors Society, P.O. Box 14013, Newark, NJ 07198

Wedgwood Society, The Roman Villa, Rockburne, Fordingbridge, Hants, England, SP6 3PB

Museums

Art Institute of Chicago, Chicago, IL

Birmingham Museum of Art, Birmingham, AL

Cincinnati Museum of Art, Cincinnati, OH

Cleveland Museum of Art, Cleveland, OH

Henry E. Huntington Library & Art Gallery, San Marino, CA

Nelson-Atkins Museum of Art, Kansas City, MO

Potsdam Public Museum, Potsdam, NY

Rose Museum, Brandeis University, Waltham, MA

R.W. Norton Art Gallery, Shreveport, LA

Wadsworth Atheneum, Hartford, CT

Dealers/Matching Services

Carol's Antique Gallery, Carol Payne, 14455 Big Basin Way, Saratoga, CA 95070, phone (408) 867-7055

Rosemary Evans, 9303 McKinney Rd., Loveland, OH 45140

Lydia's Antiques, P.O. Box 462, Newbury Park, CA 91319, phone (805) 496-7805

Olympus Cove Antiques & China, 179 E. 300 S., Salt Lake City, UT 84111, phone (800) 284-8046

Past & Presents Replacements, 65-07 Fitchett St., Rego Park, NY 11374, phone (718) 897-5515

Porcelains Ltd, P.O. Box 892, Devon, PA 19333, phone (215) 296-0550

Seal Simons, 473 W. Ellet St., Philadelphia, PA 19119, phone (215) 247-2062

Silver Lane, P.O. Box 322, San Leandro, CA 94577, phone (415) 483-0632

White's Collectables, P.O. Box 680, Newberg, OR 97132, phone (503) 538-7421

Zucker's Fine Gifts, 151 W. 26th St., New York, NY 10001, phone (212) 989-1450

Restorers/Authorities

David Brdecko, 115 W. Virginia, McKinney, TX 75069, phone (214) 542-3739

Grady Stewart, 2019 Sansom St., Philadelphia, PA 19103, phone (215) 567-2888

Van Cline & Davenport, Ltd., Stephen Van Cline, CAPP (authority), 792 Franklin Ave., Franklin Lakes, NJ 07417, phone (201) 891-4588

Manufacturers/Producers/Distributors

Waterford Wedgwood USA Inc., P.O. Box 1454, Wall, NJ 07719, phone (201) 938-5800

Wedgwood, 41 Madison Ave., New York, NY 10010, phone (212) 532-5050

Prices

Wedgwood is a blue chip antique in the American antiques market – a pleasure to collect and a sound investment.

For over a century, Wedgwood has enjoyed a strongly devoted collector base. American collectors are research oriented and have a command of their subject far in excess of that found among American collectors in many other antiques categories.

American collectors do not collect in isolation. They are an integral part of the international Wedgwood market. Major American collectors and their primary dealers frequently travel to England to scour the antiques shops and dealers' showrooms, and to actively bid at auction houses.

American Wedgwood prices vary. A number of pieces trade within a narrow range of plus or minus 10 to 20 percent of perceived "fair market" value. Wedgwood, from rarities to above average pieces, appear regularly in the pottery and porcelain auctions of American auction houses such as Skinner and Sotheby's.

Peter Williams' *Wedgwood* is an excellent introduction to Wedgwood wares. The illustrations show the finest pieces available in each category. Many of these objects are from museum collections and not readily available on the market. In order to introduce collectors to the wide variety of Wedgwood objects available in the American marketplace, it is more apropos to provide an introductory price guide to Wedgwood rather than a price guide to the items illustrated in this book.

Prices vary widely depending on who is in attendance at a Wedgwood auction, region of country, and level of experience of dealer. The following prices assume a fine to perfect condition unless noted otherwise. The prices given do not relate directly to any objects held in specific collections, and in particular do not represent the views of Wedgwood Ltd.

Wedgwood Price Listings

BLACK BASALT
(1768-)

BOWL, 4⅜" d, 2⅜" h, classical scenes, impressed mark reading "WEDGWOOD" 20th C. $25.00

BOX, cover, 7⅞" d, circular, bronzed relief dec on sides, six classical vignettes enclosed by gilt anthemia and acanthus borders, cover with bronzed figures from "Domestic Employment" within a gilt floral border, impressed mark reading "WEDGWOOD," c1880 $850.00

BUST
4¼" h, Aristophanes, impressed mark reading "WEDGWOOD" $500.00

13¾" h, Joseph Addison, modeled full head to mid chest, impressed title "Addison" on back, impressed mark reading "Wedgwood and Bentley" both bust and raised circular base, c1775 $4,500.00

14" h, John Bunyan, black, raised circular base, impressed uppercase marks, 19th C. $1,000.00

14¾" h, Horace, modeled with head turned slightly to the right, waisted circular socle, bust impressed

"HORACE WEDGWOOD," socle impressed "WEDGWOOD," circular potter's mark, date cipher AFF for April 1877 $1,000.00

17" h, 10¼" d, Mercury, black, impressed mark reading "WEDGWOOD" $2,500.00

18¼" h, Mercury, black, looking to left, winged helmet, named on reverse, socle base, impressed mark reading "WEDGWOOD," mid 19th C. $2,500.00

CANDLESTICKS, pr
4¾" h, applied relief with classical figures and trees, flaring feet with scrolling flowering foliage, impressed marks, mustache and number 5, c1850 $575.00

8¼" h, dolphin, upward tail, leafy molded sconces, rectangular base, shell border, minor repairs, impressed mark reading "WEDGWOOD," late 18th C. $1,300.00

COFFEEPOT, 9¼" h, basketweave, Widow Warburton finial $375.00

CREAMER
2¾" h, black, one side classic figural scene of old man with serpent and

young man with dish in his hand, reverse side classical figure of old woman washing young woman's feet $150.00

3⅛" h, bulbous base, straight neck, black, hand painted enameled crest of Ontario, green maple leaf, side trim, orange Ontario banner underneath, green enamel rim and handle trim, marked "Wedgwood, England" and painter's number $150.00

EGYPTIAN PLAQUE, 8 x 8½", black, hand gilded panel scene of King Tut and Queen Ankhesenamun, titled "The Beloved of the Great Enchantress," metal fitted for hanging, limited edition of 250, numbered 195, impressed and gilt marks, 1974 $600.00

EWER, 17¼" h, entwined handle and neck molded as sea god riding dolphin's head, molded sea foliage on body, leaf tip molded base, fluted socle, impressed mark reading "WEDGWOOD" $1,500.00

FIGURE
2⅞" h, 4⅝" l, bulldog, impressed mark reading "WEDGWOOD" $500.00

3½" h, 4¾" l, elephant, impressed mark reading "WEDGWOOD" $750.00

3½" h, 5" l, elephant, walking, yellow glass eyes, white jasper tusks, "WEDGWOOD MADE IN ENGLAND" mark, c1919 $750.00

4½" l, nude sleeping child on blanket, rectangular base, impressed mark reading "WEDGWOOD" $1,800.00

5½" h, squirrel, holding nut, glass eyes, impressed mark, c1915, one leg restored $500.00

7¼" h, bison, standing pose, molded grass between legs, irregular shaped rectangular base, sgd "Skeaping," c1927 $880.00

11" h, Nymph at Well, female figure holding shell, seated on shaped oval base, inscribed title, impressed mark, c1840 $1,045.00

11¾" h, Bacchus, scantily draped in goat skin, wearing foliage in hair, carrying foliage branch on circular tree stump base, applied fruiting vine, base with band of oak leaves, impressed mark, late 19th C. $1,000.00

Poor Maria, modeled, seated on rockwork base, right arm supported on tree stump suspending her hat, dog by her side held by ribbon, circular base, minor chip to cloak, titled "Sternes Poor Maria," impressed mark at reverse, 19th C. $1,350.00

INKSTAND, 3¾" h, urn shaped quill holder with double handles ending in double sides stand, circular inkwell and sander with molded shell motif on cover, impressed mark reading "WEDGWOOD," late 18th C. $1,870.00

JARDINIERE, 4½" h, cylindrical, applied high relief with lion's masks suspending fruiting vine above cameos of classical figure, rims with bands of flowering and fruiting foliage, impressed mark and numerals, c1840, pair $850.00

LAMP, oil, cover
5½" h, whale tail, cover applied in relief with Cupid unmasked within

band of oak leaves and acorns, impressed mark, late 18th C. $600.00

8¾" h, body molded with acanthus leaves, rim with band of acorns and oak leaves, top molded with shallow grooves surmounted by maiden holding jug, cover with knob finial, flaring foot, sq base, canted corners, impressed mark, mid 19th C. $825.00

Four equally spaced shell molded wick holders, interior piping intact, sq base, minor chip repair, impressed mark reading "WEDGWOOD," late 18th C. $1,200.00

MEDALLION
2" l, oval, portrait bust of Thucyd, impressed name below, impressed mark reading "WEDGWOOD & BENTLEY: ETRURIA," c1780 $350.00

4⅛" l, 3⅛" w, King George, oval 8¼ x 6¼" mahogany frame, inlaid flame satinwood liner $275.00

PENDANT, oval, black, lion chasing horses, beaded starling silver frame and chain $75.00

PITCHER, 4¾" h, tankard shape, black, classical women and childrens scene, grape and vine border, large mark with "8" in circle $155.00

PLAQUE, 7⅜" h, 5½" w, oval shape, Hercules and two headed boar, impressed mark reading "WEDGWOOD" $1,000.00

TEA CUP AND SAUCER, bronzed and gilt classical figures within ovals divided by amatory and musical trophies suspended from ribbons and foliage swags, rim chip to saucer, impressed mark, c1840 $900.00

URN, cover, 11" h, pedestal, sq base, swags, acanthus leaves at base and cover, c1860 $1,700.00

VASE
6¾" h, cover, serpent handles terminating in male masks, classical female reliefs on either side, mounted on square base, handles restored, cover replacement, circular stamp mark on base, c1775 $2,200.00

7" h, acanthus molded loop handles, cherubs representing Seasons on either side, fluting to neck and socle, mounted on sq base, circular stamp mark on base, c1775 $1,500.00.

7¾" h, cover, urn shape, high relief floral swags suspended from rams heads enclosing flowerhead motifs, knob finial, scroll handles, foliage motif, sq pedestal, impressed mark reading "WEDGWOOD & BENTLEY: ETRURIA" within circle, 1770–80 $1,500.00

9¼" h, cover, loop handles, bead trim with zodiac border above scenes of children, sq base, impressed mark reading "WEDGWOOD AND BENTLEY" on base, c1775 $2,400.00

9¾" h, beaker, slender flaring bodies, applied trailing vines suspended from ovals with amatory and sporting trophies, lower parts with formal leaves, flaring feet with fruiting vines, one minor rim chip, impressed marks, 19th C., pair $825.00

10" h, 5" d, cupids on panther driven chariot, ram driven chariot on other side, grape dec handles, marked "Wedgwood" $825.00

13⅞" h, cover, engine turned fluted neck and foot, satyr's mask and snake handles, body dec on one side in high relief with Erato and Cupid, sq base, later married cover with ball knob, impressed circular mark reading "WEDGWOOD & BENTLEY : ETRURIA," c1769-80 $2,475.00

14⅛" h, cover, satyr's mask and snake handles, body dec on one side in high relief with Erato and Cupid, sq base, composition cover with ball knob, impressed wafer mark reading "WEDGWOOD & BENTLEY: ETRURIA," c1769-80 $2,750.00

16½" h, engine turned fluted body, shoulder dec with band of berried laurel, two leopard's head and foliate bask handles, foot with foliate border, sq base with minor chips, ankle chipped, impressed circular mark reading "WEDGWOOD & BENTLEY: ETRURIA," c1775 $3,850.00

17" h, Pegasus, one with Apotheosis of Homer, other with Apothesis of Vergil, after designs by John Flaxman, snake handles issuing from Medusa's masks, covers surmounted by Pegasus on cloud scrolls, flaring feet and lower parts with palmettes and acanthus, cylindrical necks with band of laurel, impressed mark reading "WEDGWOOD" and potter's marks, 19th C., matched pair $5,500.00

20¾" h, oviform, applied dec of Apollo and the Muses, shoulder and foot with band of overlapping leaves below formal foliage, lower part with acanthus, cover with vase finial applied with formal foliage, plain loop handles, minor chips to applied decoration, impressed mark reading "WEDGWOOD," 19th C. $1,870.00

WINE EWER
16" h, figural models by John Flaxman on shoulders, swags of vine and water reeds, stiff leaves, bands of overlapping foliage, gadrooned stems, sq bases, impressed mark, c1860, pair $3,000.00

17¼" h, entwined handle and neck molded as satyr riding ram's head, molded berried vine on body, leaf tip molded base, fluted socle, impressed mark reading "WEDGWOOD" $1,500.00

BONE CHINA
(1812-1822, 1878-)

BOUGH POT, cover, 14¾" h, Eastern Flowers pattern, blue floral motif, gilt trim, yellow ground, pierced lid, first period, pair $2,500.00

CUP AND SAUCER
Blue and gilt, trailing oak leaves and acorns, iron-red printed and impressed marks, late 19th C. $110.00

Molded with overlapping vine leaves and gilt rims, iron-red printed and impressed marks, late 19th C. $125.00

DISH, 9¾" l, oval, view of Cottage at Pinxton within gilt rim, c1815 $485.00

MILK PITCHER, 6⅜" h, hexagonal, Imari palette, c1880 $225.00

TEA SERVICE, partial, 7¼" w cylindrical teapot, covered creamer, two handled covered sugar bowl, four cups and saucers, Kashmir pattern, printed and painted in iron-red black and yellow, iron-red printed Portland vase and Wedgwood marks, impressed marks, c1880 $850.00

CANE WARE
(1770-1940)

BOWL, drabware dec of ferns and stars, c1810 $425.00

BULB Pot, 8½" l, D shape, engine turned basketwork, ropework borders, glazed interior, cover with three bulb holders, nine small circular apertures, impressed mark, c1800 $1,500.00

DISH, 9¾" l, rectangular, molded with overlapping leaves, impressed mark, letter "L", c1790 $250.00

FRUIT STAND, 12⅜" d, foliate scroll handles, rectangular flaring foot, impressed mark reading "Wedgwood," early 19th C. $350.00

GAME PIE DISH, cover, 9¾" l, oval, glazed interior, exterior with relief dec, six groups of pendant game birds, and grapevine festoons, four game groups on cover, rabbit knob, crack and interior chip $225.00

PASTRY DISH, cover, 12" l, matching undertray, piecrust rim, relief molded, lattice and acanthus leaf dec, c1800 $650.00

POTPOURRI VASE, 8¾" h, 7" d, 10" w, grapevine pattern, square base, impressed mark reading "WEDGWOOD" $650.00

SOLITAIRE SET, 5" covered teapot, covered sugar bowl, milk jug, tea cup and saucer, tray, enameled garden flowers, blue line borders, glazed interior, impressed mark, c1820 $1,000.00

SUGAR BOWL, cover
4½" h, 4" d, cherubs, impressed mark, reading "WEDGWOOD" $230.00

6" h, smear glaze, prunus blossoms, c1800 $300.00

TEA CADDY SPOON, 3" l, shell shaped bowl, upper lower case mark, c1790 $550.00

TEAPOT, cover
4" h, pentagonal, molded cluster of bamboo stalks, inset cover, coiled bamboo sprig knob, impressed mark reading "Wedgwood & Bentley," c1779 $3,100.00

4¼" h, beehive, molded with horizontal bands of bound reds, applied raffia bound scroll handle and tapering spout, repaired handle, c1800 $1,000.00

6¾" w, oval, dark brown applied relief of domestic employment figures, radiating acorns and oak leaves on cover, repair to tip of spout and cover, impressed mark reading "WEDGWOOD," c1810 $550.00

VASE, 8¾" h, sq, pierced domed lid, concave sides, relief brown classical figures, brown foliage caryatid corner supports suspending swags, four brown paw feet, stepped shaped sq base, impressed mark, c1800 $1,200.00

WASTE BOWL, 5½" d, Wicker pattern, impressed mark, c1820 $100.00

CREAM WARE
(aka QUEEN'S WARE)
(MADE 1759-   )

ARGYLE, 5" h, loop handle, swan neck spout, impressed upper case mark, cover missing, nick on spout, late 18th C. $750.00

BASKET
9" d, round, reticulated, c1790 $200.00

10⅞" l, matching 12" l undertray, oval, green striped rims, loop handles $250.00

CALENDAR TILES, made between 1879 and 1929, price depends on condition and scene, prices range fro $40.00 to $200.00 with the rarest tiles bringing $450.00
   1878, King's Chapel, Boston, Wedgwood Etruria England mark $150.00

COMPOTE, 8¼" d, 4¾" h, basketweave, reticulated foliate scroll, rope twist rim handles $175.00

DISH, 10¼" w, oval, painted in colors by F. H. Cox, clusters of fruit, transfer printed rims in green with scrolling flowering branches, gilt rims, sgd by Cox, impressed marks and date letters, brown pattern #G4744, c1880, pair $300.00

FIGURE, 7" h, 4⅞" w, 10" l, polar bear, sgd "J Skeaping," c1927 $650.00

FOOD MOLD, jelly, 9" h, conical, painted, rose, purple, green, yellow, blue, and iron-red floral sprays and swags, bow knotted ribbons, brown line borders, four apertures on base, impressed mark reading "Wedgwood" and "D," c1800, chips $2,750.00

FRUIT BOWL, oval, wide brown and plum border pattern $550.00

MINIATURE, dish, 3½" w, oval, painted in colors, apple pickers scene, brown rim, sgd "E Lessore," impressed mark, date letter for 1862 $400.00

MONTIETH, 12¾" w handle to handle, heavily scalloped rim, leaf molded handles, impressed upper case mark, 19th C. $550.00

PITCHER, 8¼" h, black transfer print, yellow and green enamel, hunt scene on one side inscribed "Stag Chase through the Thames," reverse with drinking scene under banner inscribed "Sportsman Festival," hunting verse below, stag and doe beneath spout and handle, impressed mark with two potter's marks, late 18th C. $1,600.00

PLATE, 9½" d, fable, maroon, ochre, green, and yellow, two jugs floating down stream, Spanish shaped rim, ochre and brown edges, impressed mark, sgd "E Lessore," c1865 $500.00

PLATTER, 16½" l, armorial, Duke of Clarence service, blue scallop and gilt loop border, impressed upper case marks, c1816, pair $750.00

SAUCE DISH, cover, attached underplate, oval, two handles, glazed $250.00

SERVING DISH, 11¾" l, shaped rectangular, brown edged scalloped rim, low relief interior molded with two fish, small painted swan below banner, inscribed "AI SIDERA VULTUS," impressed mark reading "Wedgwood," minor chips $200.00

SOCK BLOCK, 4¾" h, molded as child's foot, impressed mark reading

"Wedgwood," letter "J," dated cipher, c1890 $250.00

SOUP TUREEN, cover, 17" w, painted with bands of flowering foliage in blue and green between black lines, handles with foliate terminals, cover with flowerhead finial, small chip to finial, impressed mark, letter "K," black pattern #1313, c1810 $400.00

SUGAR BOWL, cover, stand, 8" w, painted with bands of flowering foliage, iron-red, green, blue, and yellow, cover with disc finial and flowerhead motif, impressed marks, iron-red pattern #1173, c1860 $350.00

TEA CADDY, cover, 13 cm h, arched, transfer printed, painted in colors, birds and flowering branches dec, cover with knob finial, impressed mark reading "Wedgwood," c1820 $400.00

TEAPOT
5¼" h, globular, foliage molded spout and handle, painted loose bunches of flowers and scattered leaves, band of iron-red circlets with purple flowers, pierced ball finial, attributed to David Rhodes, c1775 $1,650.00

9" h, swelled cylindrical, dome cover, knop finial, brown dec, circular band and floral sprigs, scrolling vines, impressed mark reading "Wedgwood" $250.00

TRAY, 6¼" w, diamond shaped, transfer printed and painted in colors by Emil Lessore, scene of embracing Cupids among clouds, ochre rim, signed with reversed interlaced initials "EL," impressed mark and letters "C," "AVO," c1865 $550.00

TUREEN, cover, 17" l, Neo-classical, painted sepia dec, loop handles, fitted undertray, early 19th C. $650.00

TUREEN, cover, stand, brown Water Lily pattern, floral finial, gilt handles, impressed mark, c1810 $1,450.00

URN, 6" h, cover mottled blue and brown, glazed, mounted on basalt plinth, marked "Wedgwood and Bentley," c1768-80 $1,800.00

WATER SET, 4 pcs, pitcher, two tumblers, and tray, dog handles, gilt, Victorian $550.00

WINE COOLER, puce scalloped rim edged with gilded darts, fluted handles, bacchic trophies, impressed mark reading "Wedgwood" and "D" in gold, one handle repaired, c1790 $500.00

DRAB WARE
(1774-   )

BOWL, 7" d, 3⅝" h, basketweave pattern, flared lip, impressed mark reading "WEDGWOOD" $200.00

CREAMER, 2½" h, 5" w, light brown, c1840 $175.00

CUP AND SAUCER, applied blue bands of flowering foliage $100.00

JUG, 8" h, classical women emb on panels, loop handle, Wedgwood mark, c1820 $225.00

PITCHER, 6⅜" h, six panels, relief ladies and scrollwork $195.00

TEA SET, 3½" h teapot, covered sugar bowl, milk jug, waste bowl, basketweave, button knobs, impressed mark, early 19th C. $275.00

TEAPOT, 8½″ h, Gothic dec, bearded man faces on lower section, impressed mark reading "Wedgwood" $225.00

VASE, 10″ h, blue and white, three sections, figural swan handles $400.00

JASPER
(1774-   )

BISCUIT JAR, cover
5½″ h, yellow and black, classical figures $725.00

6″ h, yellow and white, acorn cover $575.00

6″ h, 5¼″ d, solid dark blue jasper ground, white classical ladies dec, silver plated top and rim, marked "Wedgwood, England" $250.00

7″ h, 5¼″ d, solid dark blue jasper ground, white relief of classical lady and Cupids, resilvered top, ball footed base, marked "WEDGWOOD, ENGLAND" $225.00

7¾″ h, lavender ground, white floral dec, acorn finial, artist sgd "Barnard" $710.00

9″ w handle to handle, sage green ground, white classic cameos, lavender bands at top and bottom, silver plated handle and rim $925.00

BOWL, 4½″ d, solid blue jasper ground, white relief classical dancing figures, grape leaf swag, lion's heads border $65.00

BROOCH, 1¾ x 3¼″, solid dark blue jasper ground, white relief of Psyche, oval convex shape, brass frame and jeweling, polished edge, impressed upper case mark $275.00

BUTTER DISH, cover, 4″ h, 7″ d, solid dark blue jasper ground, raised white classical figures, silver plated lid and plate, marked "Wedgwood" $165.00

BUTTONS, set of 5, solid dark blue jasper ground, cut steel mounts, attributed to Matthew Boulton, late 18th C., framed $500.00

CANDLESTICKS, pair
6¼″ h, solid blue jasper ground, white coat of arms of St. Andrews, inscribed name and motto, scrolling foliage, circular column, flaring feet, impressed marks $325.00

10¼″ h, figural, Ceres and Cybele, light green ground, white raised dec, each holding cornucopia, leaf molded sconce, standing on circular platforms mounted on sq bases, uppercase impressed marks, c1800 $1,400.00

CHANDELIER DISH, 10¾″ d, light blue jasper ground, applied white classical panels, chips at mounting hole, impressed mark, late 19th C. $470.00

CHEESE DISH, cover, 9¼″ d, dark blue jasper grond, white classical cameos, domed cover, impressed mark reading "WEDGWOOD, ENGLAND" $650.00

CHIMNEY PIECE TABLETS, 22½″ h, 5¾″ w, and 10¼″ h, 5¾″ h, white jasper relief, one with bow tied ribbed suspending classical ewer and scabbard hung with floral wreath, other with flaming pedestal hung with floral swags, green body, framed, and glazed, late 18th C. $4,250.00

CLOCK, 9¼ x 6¾″, light green ground, white relief classical figures $800.00

COFFEE CAN AND SAUCER, 2½″ h, light blue ground, applied lilac medallions and white trophies, rams' heads, and floral garlands, impressed upper case marks, 19th C. $1,250.00

COMPOTE, 7¾″ d, 9½″ d underplate, yellow, applied grapevine borders, added central acanthus leaves, impressed marks, c1890, minor interior stain ring $825.00

CUP AND SAUCER, three color, green ground, white relief rams' heads suspending floral swags enclosing oval medallions of classical figures on lilac ground, impressed marks, 19th C. $1,200.00

FLOWER POT, 7⅞″ h, solid blue jasper ground, white relief of Cupid as Four Seasons, each Cupid in niche flanked by palm trees, shaped rim, floral and foliate border, fluted base with guilloche band, four paterae-dec feet, chips to feet, cover missing, impressed mark reading "WEDGWOOD" and letter "V," c1785 $850.00

HAIR RECEIVER, cover, heart shape, medium blue ground, large white angel dec, numbered only $250.00

JARDINIERE, 10¼″ d, 8¾″ h, bulbous, olive green ground, white applied classical relief, impressed mark reading "England," c1920 $415.00

JUG, 6¼″ h, pear shaped, red jasper dip ground, white relief with classical figures and Cupid between bands of flowerheads, loop handle with anthemion, impressed mark reading "Made in England," early 20th C. $800.00

LOVING CUP, 4½″ h, three handles, olive green ground, white cameo medallions of Washington, Franklin, and Lafayette, marked "Wedgwood, England" $450.00

MANTLE LUSTERS, 11½″ h, cylindrical, light blue and white jasper base, silver plated mounts, relief dec of cupids, festoons and rams' heads, two center trophies and oval medallions in violet, molded and cut glass bobeche hung with drops, glass floriform nozzle, pair $3,000.00

MATCH HOLDER
2″ h, solid black jasper ground, white relief of classical figures and Psyche being bound by Cupids below band of scrolling flowering foliage, impressed mark $175.00

2⅛″ h, black dip ground, white relief portrait of Shakespeare and Josiah Wedgwood, names inscribed below on ribbon, date 1730-1795, impressed mark reading "Museum" and date 1906 $165.00

MEDALLION, PORTRAIT
1⅞″ h, 1½″ w, oval, solid blue jasper ground, white relief bust of Frederick William II, King of Prussia, brass frame, impressed mark reading "Wedgwood and Bentley," c1780 $550.00

4½″ h, 2⅜″ w, solid blue jasper ground, white relief bust of Benjamin Franklin and Lafayette, impressed mark reading "WEDGWOOD," pair $150.00

MINIATURE, pitcher, 2½″ h, crimson dip ground, bulbous, white relief classical figures, impressed mark and "Made In England," c1920 $550.00

MUG, 5″ h, 3¾″ d, dark blue jasper ground, raised white classical figures, rope handle, raised white medallion, silver plated rim $145.00

PITCHER
6″ h, light blue ground, white cameos of maidens, peacock, cherubs, trees, and floral bouquet $150.00

7½″ h, olive green ground, white relief medallions of Franklin and Hamilton, "WEDGWOOD, ENGLAND" mark $350.00

7¾″ h, sage green jasper ground, classical figures, cupid, and cherubs, marked "Wedgwood, England" $85.00

8¼″ h, olive green ground, white classical cameos, rope twist handle, impressed mark reading "WEDGWOOD, ENGLAND" $220.00

PLAQUE
8¼″ l, 5⅞″ h, solid blue ground, white cameos of marriage of Cupid and Psyche $650.00

8⅝″ l, 3½″ h, black ground, white cameos of five classical figures in theatrical setting, impressed mark reading "WEDGWOOD" $350.00

12″ l, 6″ h, rectangular, central panel of light blue jasper, white relief cameos of Dancing Hours, applied white leaf border, light green outer border, impressed "Wedgwood" only, hairline crazing, c1840 $1,500.00

16″ l, 5½″ h, light blue ground, white relief depicting "The Body of Hector Dragged at the Car of Achilles," carved oak frame, impressed mark $1,210.00

20¾″ l, 6¼″ h, blue ground, white cameos of Achilles in Syros among the daughters of Lycomedes, impressed mark reading "WEDGWOOD" $1,330.00

26″ l, 9½″ h, solid blue ground, white relief of Sacrifice to Love, figures bringing ox and flowers to Cupid on altar, impressed mark reading "WEDGWOOD" $2,300.00

POTPOURRI VASE, cover
12⅝″ h, green dip ground, white relief with four classical medallions between rams' heads suspending floral swags, sq base with anthemia flanked flowerheads, pierced cover with anthemia and acanthus leaves, repaired cover, impressed mark reading "WEDGWOOD," late 19th or early 20th C. $750.00

13¾″ h, three color, green dip ground, white relief with four classical medallions within yellow beadwork borders between white rams' heads tied with yellow ribbons suspending white floral garlands above yellow and white floral, foliate, beadwork, twisted cable, and rope-twist borders, sq base with white anthemia flanked flowerheads, pierced cover with yellow acanthus and anthemion motifs, surface cracks on base, impressed mark reading "WEDGWOOD" and potter's mark, late 19th C. $990.00

PRESERVE JAR, 6″ h, cover, solid dark blue jasper ground, matching underplate, four classical Muses in cartouches, marked "Wedgwood, England" $200.00

RING TREE, 2¾″ h, center post, solid blue jasper ground, panels of white cameos of classical ladies, floral border, WEDGWOOD mark $145.00

SCENT BOTTLE, solid dark blue jasper ground, white relief ⅜″ classical figures on each side, 19th C. $675.00

SWEETMEAT, cover, 3¼″ h, cylindrical, solid dark blue jasper

ground, white horses and figures, knob finial, marked "Wedgwood" $185.00

TEA CADDY, 5¾″ h, cover yellow ground, white and black classical figures, marked "WEDGWOOD, ENGLAND" $1,000.00

TEAPOT, cover
5¼″ h, 5⅘″ d, sage green ground, white raised classical figures, marked "Wedgwood England" $195.00

5½″ h, Empire shape, solid blue ground, white relief with "Sportive Love" on one side, figures from "Domestic Employment" on other, cover and base with engine turned flutes, overpainted hair crack, small chips, repaired knob, impressed mark reading "WEDGWOOD" and number "3," c1790 $440.00

TEA SET, 7¾″ h covered teapot, creamer, covered sugar, solid dark blue jasper ground, white classical figures, impressed mark reading "England" $450.00

TOOTHPICK HOLDER, 2¼″ h, dark blue jasper ground, white bust of Josiah Wedgwood, marked "Wedgwood, Made In England" $125.00

URN, cover
7½″ h, three color, white ground, green swags and acanthus leaves, lilac rams' masks, two green medallions with white classical figures on lilac ground, floral lilac shoulder band, flared foot, ball finial, scroll handles, impressed mark, mid 19th C. $1,500.00

VASE
3¾″ h, Strapware, white ground, lilac and green, base crazed, upper case mark $600.00

7¼″ h, three color, white jasper ground, applied in relief with foliage swags and acanthus leaves in green jasper suspended from lilac jasper rams' masks, shoulder with band of flowerheads within entwined ribbons, body applied with two medallions depicting classical figures on lilac ground within green jasper surround, lower part with anthemion and flowers in green and lilac, flaring foot with band of foliage, cover with ball finial, handles repaired, impressed mark reading "WEDGWOOD" and number "2," mid 19th C. $800.00

7½″ h, three color, light green dip to upper and lower body, light blue central panel, white classical relief, stiff leaf borders, scrolled handles, staining, one handle damaged, c1860 $440.00

9¾″ h, white ground, lilac and green relief, oval medallions of classical subjects within rams' heads draped by floral garlands, impressed upper case mark, early 19th C. $800.00

10″ h Portland Vase, 19th-C. copy, blue dip ground, white relief with continuous frieze of classical figures said to represent the myth of Pelius and Thetis. White base with half-length figure wearing Phrygian cap, small chip to relief, impressed mark reading "WEDGWOOD" $2,500.00

Urn shape, cover, pale blue jasper dip ground, white relief with flowering foliage swags suspended from rams' head to the shoulder, horns forming handles, shoulder with band of ribbon entwined foliage, body applied with two cameos depicting classical figures on lavender ground, lower part and cover with stiff leaves, flaring foot and sq base with anthemion, impressed mark reading "WEDGWOOD," mid 19th C. $1,800.00

10¼" h, dark blue jasper ground, loop handles, applied white relief of trophies over continuous frieze of classical figures, minor relief loss, impressed mark reading "Made in England," c1800 $850.00

10½" h, three color, dipped ground, "The Dancing Hours" on rose ground, shoulder, lower part and foot with formal foliage and anthemion on blue ground, bearded mask handles, chip to interior of cover and small chip to foot, impressed mark reading "Wedgwood, England," early 20th C. $1,200.00

11¼" h, solid blue jasper ground, white relief with foliage swags suspended from paterae tied with ribbons and two oval medallions enclosing classical figures, sides with sporting trophies below the handles, lower part with foliage, cover with oak leaves and acorns and vase finial, rim with band of fruiting foliage, repair to finial, impressed mark reading "WEDGWOOD" and mustache mark, early 19th C. $900.00

11¾" h, three color, green dip ground, white relief with sacrifice scene on either side between dice pattern borders with vertical rows of berried laurel branches alternating with green and white checkered squares and blue flowerheads, foot with foliate border, blue married cover with white stiff leaves and palmettes, repaired foot chips, impressed mark reading "WEDGWOOD," letter "H," and potter's mark, late 19th C. $1,200.00

13" h, three color, black dip ground, white relief with continuous frieze of putti at various pursuits above wide section of dice pattern and vertical rows of interlaces circlets alternating with black and white checkered squares with yellow flowerheads, foot with foliate border, cover with arch enclosed florets and lilies, repaired cover, impressed mark reading "WEDGWOOD," letter "J," and potter's mark, 19th C. $3,025.00

13¼" h, turquoise dip ground, white relief on either side with putti vintners below grapevine band, between egg and dark, gadroon, laurel, and foliate borders, sq base with anthemia flanked flowerheads, cover with alternating stiff leaves and palmettes, repaired base, hair crack in foot, impressed mark reading "WEDGWOOD" and number "2," c1880 $440.00

13¾" h, three color, blue dip ground, white relief on one side with "Bellerophon Watering Pegasus," and "The Archers" on other, within lilac-ground border of zodiac symbols, beneath foliate garland pendant from ribbons and paterae, ribbon tied wings, band of stiff leaves below, cover rim with ribbon entwined ivy vine surrounding Cupid knop, sides with white Medusa-mask and serpent handles, sq base with scrollwork, one handle repaired, impressed mark reading "WEDGWOOD," mid 19th C. $1,350.00

16⅜" h, crimson dip ground, white relief on vase and pedestal with classical portrait medallions between bow-tied swags of fruiting grapevines, cover with still leaves and pierced flowerheads, repaired cover chip, unmarked, c1928 $2,500.00

LIMITED EDITIONS

CALENDAR SERIES PLATES

1971, Victorian Almanac, first edition $20.00

1972, The Carousel $15.00

1973, Bountiful Butterfly $14.00

1974, Camelot $65.00

1975, Children's Games $18.00

1976, Robin $25.00

1977, Tonatiuh $28.00

1978, Samuari $32.00

1979, Sacred Scarab $32.00

1980, Safari $40.00

1981, Horses $40.00

1982, Wild West $42.50

1983, The Age of the Reptiles $50.00

1984, Dogs $55.00

1985, Cats $55.00

1986, British Birds $50.00

1987, Water Birds $50.00

1988, Sea Birds $50.00

CHRISTMAS ORNAMENTS, jasper stoneware

1988, Christmas Tree, first edition $28.00

1989, Angel $28.00

1990, Santa Claus $28.00

1991, Wreath $28.00

CHRISTMAS PLATES, jasper stoneware, 8" d

1969, Windsor Castle, first edition $225.00

1970, Christmas in Trafalgar Square $30.00

1971, Piccadilly Circus, London $40.00

1972, St Paul's Cathedral $40.00

1973, The Tower of London $45.00

1974, The Houses of Parliament $40.00

1975, Tower Bridge $40.00

1976, Hampton Court $45.00

1977, Westminster Abbey $48.00

1978, The Horse Guards $55.00

1979, Buckingham Palace $55.00

1980, St James Palace $70.00

1981, Marble Arch $75.00

1982, Lambeth Palace $80.00

1983, All Souls, Langham Palace $80.00

1984, Constitution Hill $80.00

1985, The Tate Gallery $80.00

1986, The Albert Memorial $80.00

1987, Guildhall $80.00

1988, The Observatory/Greenwich $95.00

1989, Winchester Cathedral $85.00

EASTER EGGS

1977 $35.00

1978 $25.00

1979 $18.00

1983 $40.00

MOTHER'S DAY PLATES, jasper stoneware, 6½" d

1971, Sportive Love, first edition $25.00

1972, The Sewing Lesson $20.00

1973, The Baptism of Achilles $20.00

1974, Domestic Employment $30.00

1975, Mother and Child $35.00

1976, The Spinner $35.00

1977, Leisure Time $30.00

1978, Swan and Cygnets $35.00

1979, Deer and Fawn $35.00

1980, Birds $48.00

1981, Mare and Foal $50.00

1982, Cherubs with Swing $55.00

1983, Cupid and Butterfly $55.00

1984, Musical Cupids $55.00

1985, Cupids and Doves $55.00

1986, Cupids Fishing $55.00

1987, Spring Flowers $80.00

1988, Tiger Lily $55.00

1989, Irises $65.00

1991, Peonies $65.00

NEW YEAR BELL

1979, Penguins, first edition $48.00

1981, Polar Bears $50.00

1982, Moose $35.00

1983, Fur Seals $32.00

1984, Ibex $50.00

1985, Puffin $60.00

1986, Ermine $60.00

QUEEN'S CHRISTMAS PLATES, A. Price artist

1980, Windsor Castle $30.00

1981, Trafalgar Square $25.00

1982, Piccadilly Circus $35.00

1984, Tower of London $35.00

1985, Palace of Westminster $35.00

1986, Tower Bridge $35.00

LUSTRE WARES (FROM 1806)

BUTTERFLY

BOWL

2¾ x 1¾", octagonal, gold outlined multicolored butterflies, gold trim, mottled mother of pearl luster exterior, mottled flame interior, Portland vase mark $250.00

6½" d, flame exterior, cobalt blue interior $500.00

8" d, burgundy exterior, gilt butterflies, Oriental landscape scenes, central lotus blossom, and butterflies interior, gilt mark, painted number $900.00

8⅝" d, orange speckled interior with gold butterflies, border with cartouche and rust Oriental pagoda, exterior with pale blue irid blue butterflies, gold printed "WEDGWOOD" mark $895.00

MUG, 2" h, three handles, blue, tan, and pink, gold butterflies, coral interior, marked "Wedgwood Lustre" $300.00

PUNCH BOWL, 11" d, 6" h, white pearl exterior, coral interior, large gold butterflies, Portland vase mark, Z4832 $1,100.00

VASE

5" h, Butterfly, four multicolored butterflies on ivory luster ground, orange interior, gold neck $350.00

8⅜" h, 4⅛" d, mother of pearl luster exterior, multicolored, gold outlined butterflies, gold rim, flame luster interior, Portland vase mark $900.00

DRAGON

BOWL

4" d, blue scale exterior, gilt dec of man on camel on interior, gold interior border, printed "WEDGWOOD" mark $300.00

4½" d, 2½" h, mottled deep blue luster exterior, gold dragons, Oriental motif, mother of pearl luster interior, Portland vase mark $325.00

8¾" w, octagonal, blue exterior, yellow-green interior, printed mark, c1925, slight interior wear $700.00

9" w, octagonal, orange exterior, purple with mottled blue interior, printed mark, c1925 $800.00

BOX, cover, 5⅜" d, 5¼" h, mottled green luster interior, gold dragons $750.00

GARNITURE SET, 11" h center vase, two 8" h sq vases, flying cranes and dragon breathing flames, 3 pcs $2,000.00

SALT, 2¼" h, orange dog's head in bowl, blue exterior $130.000

URN, cover 11¼" h, magenta and gilt dec, "WEDGWOOD" mark $895.00

VASE

8" h, 3⅞" d, mottled deep blue luster exterior, gold dragons, mother of pearl interior, Portland vase mark $600.00

8¾" h, shape #2355, mixed blues, mother of pearl interior, printed marks, c1925, pair $1,750.00

FAIRYLAND

BOWL

5" d, ftd, gilt and yellow dec, playful hobgoblins on blue and green ground, gilt Portland vase and Wedgwood made in England Mark, c1920 $1,250.00

7½" w, Castle on a Road exterior, Bird in a Hoop interior, pattern Z5125, printed marks, c1920 $3,500.00

7¾" w, octagonal, Moorish exterior, black ground, Smoke Ribbons interior, c1920 $3,500.00

8¹⁄₁₆" d, exterior painted in tones of pink, green, magenta, black, yellow, and brown with "Garden of Paradise," interior with "Jumping Fawn" in tones of green, blue, yellow, and red-violet, foot painted with "Flaming Wheel" border on blue ground, gold over brown printed Portland "WEDGWOOD MADE IN ENGLAND Z4968," black "z" mark, c1920 $4,000.00

8⁷⁄₈" d, exterior with Poplar Trees pattern, interior with Eves and Bell Branch pattern, little folks and fairies amongst cobwebs, dark green ground, gilt details, 1920s, printed urn mark and Z4966 $3,500.00

9½" d, Poplar Trees exterior, Woodland Elves III–Feather Hat interior, pattern Z4968, printed marks, c1920 $3,500.00

10⅝" d, exterior with Poplar Trees pattern, interior with Woodland Bridge pattern, central circular medallion with mermaid holding mirror, printed Portland mark, Z4968, c1920 $3,500.00

MALFREY POTS, 7½" h, Flame Fairyland, shape #2311, Willow pattern Z5360, printed S and H within stylized flowers and Portland Vase marks, c1920, pair $3,500.00

MELBA CUP, 4⁷⁄₈" d, 3½" h, green mother of pearl interior with two elves on branch, midnight luster exterior, gold stars, green grass, leapfrogging elves and fairies, Portland vase mark $1,200.00

PLAQUE, 10⅞" l, 10⅞" w Elves in a Pine Tree, little folks at leisurely pursuits in pine tree, spider in cobweb, wide blue ground, gilt border, printed Portland Vase mark and Z5154, 1920s $6,000.00

Torches, scenes of steps illuminated by fairy lights rising from lake to Easter palace, overhung with tall tree entwined by serpent and supporting bird's nest, branches hung with Chinese lanterns, several pixies and elves at play, mother of pearl luster border, printed urn mark, sgd "S. M. Makeig-Jones," Z5331, 1920 $10,000.00

PLATE, 10¾" d, elves on bridge, gold center, lacy gold fairies and florals on gold border, mottled blue back $2,500.00

TRAY, 13¼" d, Flight of Birds exterior, Pebble and Grass borders, green, and blue mottled ground, Fairy gondola painted on interior, gold printed Portland Vase mark, "WEDGWOOD MADE IN ENGLAND Z49468" and red arrow marks, c1920 $3,630.00

VASE
7⅞" h, Butterfly Women, winged maidens seated in flowering branches, midnight blue ground, flared rim with pixies and birds, Z4968, c1920 $2,500.00

8½" h, Candlemas, shape #2034, pattern Z5157, c1920 $2,400.00

8⅝" h, Chinese Lighthouse, black, orange, green, blue, pink, and gilt Chinese pagodas, bridges, and light-house, three tree tunks, Chinese lanterns, and foliage on shoulders, Portland vase mark, Z5300 $2,250.00

8¾" h, ftd trumpet, multicolored glazes, gilt dec of radiant maiden and mischievous fairies, stamped mark, incised "2357" $2,250.00

11½" h, cylindrical, Torches pattern, steps leading to palace lit by torches, serpent and elves, tree nearby, flared foot and rim, Flaming Wheel border, printed urn mark, sgd "S. M. Makeig-Jones," Z4968, 3177, c1920 $4,500.00

HUMMINGBIRD

BOWL, 8" w, octagonal, blue exterior, orange interior, printed mark, c1925 $525.00

JAR, cover, 9" h, gold outlined multicolored hummingbirds, mottled green exterior, gold trim, marked "Wedgwood" $725.00

VASE
5⅛" h, gold outlined multicolored hummingbirds, mottled blue luster ground, mottled flame luster interior $400.00

9" h, green and orange hummingbirds, speckled blue ground, gilt accents, orange luster interior $900.00

MOONLIGHT

COMPOTE, 10¼" l, Nautilus pattern, splashed pink luster, orange, ochre, and gray highlights, matching 11¼" l bi-valve stand, impressed mark, c1810 $1,500.00

GOBLET, 3¼" h, shades of pink with yellow and green splashes, gilt rim, impressed mark, c1810 $450.00

PASTILLE BURNER, 4¼" h, gold luster, leafy garlands on bowl, mounted on triple dolphin supports, impressed date "Feb 2 1805" and "Josiah Wedgwood" in upper case, cover missing $800.00

PLATE, 9¾" d, purple luster splotches, c1810 $200.00

POTPOURRI VASE, 14" h, slender ovoid body, splashed pink, orange, and gray luster, recessed inner lid with button finial, pierced domed cover with cone finial, repairs to cover and inner lid, impressed mark and letter "K", c1810 $1,500.00

TUMBLER, 2¼" h, orange and black exterior, green interior with gold creatures $255.00

ORIENTAL

BOWL, 3½" d $245.00

SILVER

CREAM jug, 4½" h, band of scrolling flowering foliage in iron-red and silver luster, impressed mark, 19th C. $125.00

MAJOLICA (1860–1910)

BOWL
9" d, 4⅛" h, white and brown, emb white seashells, rose and gold seaweed, turquoise interior, silver plated rim band, impressed mark $250.00

10½" d, ftd, Cauliflower $400.00
CREAMER, 3" h, Strawberry pattern, turquoise interior, impressed mark $160.00

FISH SERVICE, 21¼" oval platter, ten serving plates, molded with shells and crustacean on basket work molded ground, pink, yellow, brown, turquoise, and green, minor repairs, impressed marks, No. 3054, numerals, c1880 $1,250.00

GAME PIE DISH, 11" l, polychrome enamels, chick finial, molded gaming trophies between floral garlands, winged creatures, Queensware liner, impressed marks, 1868 $3,575.00

MATCH STRIKER, 5" h, green and brown, sgd $200.00
PITCHER, 8½" h, jug shape, jeweled design, turquoise interior, c1860 $350.00

PLATE, 6½" d, butterflies, florals, and fans dec $125.00

SAUCE BOAT, molded and painted in gray-green, yellow, and pink, Fan pattern, flowering prunus, glazed turquoise interior, impressed mark reading "WEDGWOOD" and date letter for 1878, painter's number, pattern number $250.00

SUGAR BOWL, 7" w, two branch handles, molded and painted in gray-green, yellow, and pink, Fan pattern, flowering prunus, glazed turquoise interior, impressed mark reading "WEDGWOOD" and date letter for 1878, painter's number, pattern number $300.00

TEAPOT, cover, 6¼" h, Bamboo pattern, impressed mark, 1871 $625.00

UMBRELLA STAND, 22" h, Aesthetic Movement, basket shape, alternating molded rows of yellow and white plaited raffia, green, brown, and blue peacock feathers, pale blue ribbon, bow knot ribbon tied at either end, interior turquoise glaze, impressed mark reading "WEDGWOOD," date cipher "AJL" (April 1883), May 25, 1881 registry mark, purple letters and pattern number $2,000.00

WATER BOTTLE, 10" h, multicolored florals, horizontal blue stripes, cream ground, 1879 $300.00

PARIAN (CARRARA) WARE (1848–1880)

BUST
11¾" h, William Shakespeare, mounted on pedestal base, dated 1864, impressed "F. M. Miller Co" and "WEDGWOOD AND SONS" $880.00

14½" h, Milton, titled, impressed "E W Wyon" and "WEDGWOOD" $600.00

15" h, Sir Walter Scott, looking to left, tartan shawl draped on shoulders, socle base, impressed "E W Wyon F" and "Scott," c1860 $675.00

FIGURE, 14⅝" h, The Strawberry Girl, standing, basket, impressed "Josiah Wedgwood & Sons, England, July 12, 1858" $1,800.00

PEARL WARE (1779–1940)

BOUGH POT
8½" h, urn shape, pierced cover, mottled brown, still leaves on pedestal base $1,000.00

9" h, pierced cover, D-shape, speckled, molded floral swags, still foliage border, gilt, impressed mark, c1810, pair $1,200.00

CHURN, cover, 9¾" h, enameled, entwined ribbon and laurel, impressed marks, c1860, restored $500.00

COMPOTE
10¾" d, Havelock pattern, floral border, impressed mark, c1840–68 $265.00

12¼" w stand, Nautilus Shell, naturalistically modeled with bands, shades of pink, yellow, and mauve, simulated coral foot, stand with

molded branch of coral to center, impressed marks, iron-red pattern #7035, c1825 $700.00

DEMITASSE CUP and Saucer $200.00
FOOD MOLD, cover, jelly, 9⅞" h, interior wedge shape, puce, yellow, purple, iron-red, green, and brown painted fruit clusters, bunch of grapes and strawberry vine on end, brown line edge border, circular base with four apertures, plain outer cover, base impressed mark reading "Wedgwood" and two J form potter's marks, c1800, base chips $3,850.00

JUG, 5¾" h, blue, scenic transfer, gold wreath with initials under spout, gold grim, impressed mark, c1820 $275.00

PLATE
7⅝" d, green and black floral decoration, green feather edge impressed mark reading "WEDGWOOD" $150.00

8⅛" d, Peony pattern, blue and white florals, blue rim, impressed mark reading "WEDGWOOD" and blue Peony mark $65.00

8½" d, shell shape, natural modeling, shades of pink, impressed upper case marks, set of 12 $660.00

PLATTER, 12¾" l, Argyle pattern, border of green–yellow leaves, turquoise ground, gold accents, impressed mark reading "WEDGWOOD," c1860 $125.00

SOUP TUREEN, cover, ladle, blue dahlias, green foliage, black rope edge, impressed mark $400.00

STAND, 9¼" w, oval, molded as overlapping leaves, russet, green, and pink highlights, impressed mark reading "WEDGWOOD," late 18th C., pair $200.00

VASE, cover, 6⅝" h, tan slip, engine turned gadroons, relief beadwork and swags, impressed mark, late 18th C. $245.00

QUEENS WARE (aka CREAM WARE) (MADE 1759–)

BOX, cover, 4 x 5", round, light blue, relief berries and vine, marked "Queens Ware, Wedgwood, England" $85.00

CHOCOLATE POT, 4" h, green leaf dec $160.00

CROCUS POT, 6" h, rectangular, bombe shape, classical motifs in oval medallion $115.00

CUP AND SAUCER, relief vintage rim border, #2223 $25.00

PLATE
8⅝" d, enameled, set of six, each with different large and small floral and foliate sprigs within feather molded rim edged in purple, shades of purple on deep cream colored body, 1769–77, set of six $750.00

9¾" d, Nautilus design, Guy Green pattern #83, green shell edge, impressed mark reading "WEDGWOOD," c1777–78 $375.00

PLATTER, oval, reticulated, marked Wedgwood" $450.00

TEA SET, Edward VIII Coronation, blue, c1937, 3 pcs $400.00

TILE
6" square
November, boy at seashore, peacock blue transfer print, white ground $125.00

Red Riding Hood and wolf, black transfer print, white ground, Crane design $125.00

8" square
Hunting dog and bird scene, brown transfer print, white ground $125.00

Puck, blue transfer print, white ground, marked "Josiah Wedgwood & Sons, Etruria" $125.00

Shakespeare's Mid-Summer Night's Dream, moth, blue transfer print, white ground $125.00

Tally Ho, man riding horse, blue transfer print, white ground $125.00

ROSSO ANTICO
(1765–1920)

BOWL, Egyptian $385.00

CANDLESTICKS, pr. 8" h, Capri, columnar, painted in Famille rose palette, flowering plants, black line rims, impressed mark and letter "D", c1840 $600.00

CREAMER
2¾" h, applied grape and vine dec $175.00

6" h, applied center black band of scrolling flowering foliage, impressed mark, mid 19th C. $225.00

CAPRI, enameled flower dec $150.00

INKWELL, 2⅝" h, Egyptian manner, sq flat base, removable ink pot insert, impressed mark, late 19th C. $605.00

JUG
3½" h, miniature, dragon in relief, blue staining $100.00

4½" h, plain, incised bands, impressed mark reading "WEDGWOOD," c1880 $185.00

6" h, pinched spout, applied black formal foliage and bellflowers, c1820 $200.00

6" w, squatty, applied relief with black band of scrolling flowering foliage, impressed mark reading "WEDGWOOD," mid 19th C. $200.00

KRATER VASE, 8½" w, applied black mythological subjects, lower part with trailing husks, handles with acanthus leaves, minor chips, early 19th C. $850.00

LAMP, oil, 5½" h, black basalt ground, rosso antico applied leaves, handle, and sunburst, molded beaded trim, early 19th C. $525.00

PLAQUE, 4¼" h, 3½" w, bust of Tiberius with underglazed white and black speckles on face, impressed mark reading "WEDGWOOD/TIBERIUS," 18th C. $900.00

SUGAR BOWL, cover, 6" w, applied black Egyptian motifs, bowl with band of stylized key pattern, crocodile finial, impressed mark reading "WEDGWOOD," early 19th C. $400.00

TEAPOT, cover
8½" w, squatty, band of hieroglyphs at shoulder, crocodile finial, 1810 $750.00

10" w, squatty, band of black Egyptian motifs above stylized key pattern, strapwork bands, crocodile finial, small repair to tip of spout, impressed mark and letter "w," c1810 $800.00

VASE, 5¼" h, Portland shape, black relief lilies and foliage, flaring rim, band of grass, angular handles, applied mask terminals, impressed mark, mid 19th C. $600.00

SPECIAL EDITIONS AND COMMEMORATIVE WARES

BOX, cov, Royalty Commemorative
5" w, heart shaped, Queen Elizabeth Silver Jubilee, white bust of Queen Elizabeth on one, Prince Philip on other, blue jasper ground, floral wreath, marked "Wedgwood," matching pair $110.00

DISH, Royalty Commemorative, Prince Charles and Lady Diana Spencer, Royal Wedding, July 29, 1981, 6" d, black and white profile portraits, multicolored decoration, marked "Wedgwood Queensware" $25.00

MUG, Royalty Commemorative
2¾" h, Prince William of Wales, gold decoration $65.00

4" h
Queen Elizabeth, multicolored decoration, lion, unicorn, crown, and cypher, marked "Eric Ravilious, Wedgwood" $250.00

Prince Andrew, Conferment of Dukedom of York, black silhouette portraits, black, gold and blue decoration, designed by Richard Guyatt, limited edition of 1,000 $200.00

4¾" h, Queen Elizabeth, black and white portrait by Snowdon, marked "Wedgwood" $150.00

PLATE
7½" d
American View
Boston Tea Party, blue transfer print, marked "Wedgwood" $65.00

Capitol, Washington, DC, blue transfer print, marked "Wedgwood" $35.00

Faneuil Hall, Cradle of Liberty, blue transfer print, marked "Wedgwood" $65.00

Fort Ticonderoga, NY, blue transfer print, marked "Wedgwood" $40.00

George Washington, blue transfer print, marked "Wedgwood" $60.00

Grant's Tomb, Riverside Drive On The Hudson, blue transfer print, marked "Wedgwood" $115.00

Green Dragon Tavern, Boston, blue transfer print, marked "Wedgwood" $60.00

Grover Cleveland, blue transfer print, marked "Wedgwood" $125.00

Hermitage, Home of Andrew Jackson, blue transfer print, marked "Wedgwood" $70.00

Independence Hall, Philadelphia, blue transfer print, marked "Wedgwood" $65.00

King's Chapel, Boston, blue transfer print, marked "Wedgwood" $40.00

Marietta College 125th Anniversary, 1960 $20.00

Mormon Temple, Utah, blue transfer print, marked "Wedgwood" $110.00

Park Street Church, Boston, blue transfer print, marked "Wedgwood" $45.00

Pike's Peak, blue transfer print, marked "Wedgwood" $65.00

Pilgrim's Exiles, blue transfer print, marked "Wedgwood" $60.00

Signing of the Declaration of Independence, blue transfer print $65.00

State House, Boston, blue transfer print $45.00

Trinity Church, Copley Square, Boston, blue transfer print, marked "Wedgwood" $45.00

Van Rennsalaer Manor House, New York, blue bell border, Albany series $45.00

Royalty Commemorative, King Edward VII Coronation, bone china, dated June 26, 1902 $150.00

9¼" d, American Views, Wellesley College, blue transfer print, white ground, c1890 $35.00

9⅞" d, American Views, "Compliments of the Railway Post Office Clerks of the First Division Convention, 1904," blue transfer print, impressed and marked "Wedgwood," also impressed with logo of postal clerks on back $65.00

10" d, American Views, St Lawrence Seaway, green transfer print $50.00

10¼" d to 10½" d, set of twelve, American Views
Columbia University, blue transfer print, marked "Wedgwood" $350.00

Harvard University, red transfer print, marked "Wedgwood" $325.00

New York University School of Education, red transfer print, marked "Wedgwood" $200.00

Yale University, blue transfer print, marked "Wedgwood" $350.00

TEA SET, Royalty Commemorative, Queen Elizabeth Coronation, teapot, creamer, and sugar, relief portraits, light blue decoration on white Queensware, marked "Wedgwood," 1953 $275.00

TILE, American Views, 6" square Adams Lean-To-House, Quincy, blue-gray transfer print, 1891 $80.00

Lee Mansion, blue transfer print, marked "Wedgwood, Etruria, England" $75.00

Massachusetts Institute of Technology, light brown transfer print, 1916 $65.00

Trinity Church, Boston, brown transfer print, 1896 $75.00

TRAY, Royalty Commemorative, Prince Charles and Lady Diana Spencer, Royal Wedding, July 29, 1981, 6" l, 3¼" w, white applied profiles and decoration, pale blue jasperware ground, marked "Wedgwood, England" $60.00

TERRA COTTA WARE
(Terra Cotta and White Jasper, 1957–1959)

ASHTRAY, 4½" d, classical dec, marked "Made in England" $35.00

BOX, heart shaped $85.00

PIN DISH, 4" l, oval, cupids playing, marked "Made in England" $30.00

TOBACCO JAR, cover, round, classical figures, marked "Wedgwood Made In England," 20th C. $200.00

VARIEGATED WARE
(1759–1965)

BARBER BOTTLE, 11" h, variegated body, applied four gilt masks, shoulder divided by bands of laurel suspending trailing vine, slender necks with four rams' head masks suspending trailing flowers, lower parts with plain leaves, flaring feet with overlapping leaves in gilt, rims entwined with ribbon, covers with gilt knob finials, impressed marks, mid 19th C., pair $2,000.00

FLOWER POT, 6¼" h, creamware body, variegated brown, beige, iron-red, and gray, rim bands of molded brickwork, flower pot restored, impressed mark reading "Wedgwood and Bentley," stand with lower case mark, c1780 $1,100.00

URN, 18⅜" h, body speckled in dark blue-green to simulate porphyry, creamware foliate handles, paterae-suspended drapery swags, bead molded rim, flame knop, heightened in touched up gilding, black basaltes base, some chips, one repaired handle, repaired knop, impressed circular mark reading "WEDGWOOD & BENTLEY: ETRURIA," c1775 $18,000.00

VASE, 15¾" h, creamware body, speckled dark blue-green, applied satyr's mask handles, one side with medallion of "Sacrifice to Aesculapius," inscribed 1502, square black basaltes base, composition cover and foot, repaired horns, impressed wafer mark reading "WEDGWOOD & BENTLEY: ETRURIA," c1769–80 $6,600.00

Index

Page numbers in *italics* refer to picture captions. **Bold** numbers refer to biographical box features.

Selected Bibliography

The American Wedgwoodian, 55 Vandam St., New York, NY 10013, USA, 1963 et seq.

ARS Ceramica, 5 Dogwood Ct., Glen Head, NY 11545

Barnard, Harry – *Chats on Wedgwood Ware,* London 1924

Batkin, Maureen – *Wedgwood Ceramics, 1846-1959,* London, 1982

Burton, William – *Josiah Wedgwood and His Pottery,* London 1922

Buten, David – *18th-Century Wedgwood,* New York, 1980

Des Fontaines, Una – *Wedgwood Fairyland Lustre,* London, 1975

Gater, Sharon and Vincent, David – *The Factory in a Garden,* Keele, 1988

Honey, W.B. – *Wedgwood Ware,* London, 1948

Josiah Wedgwood: the Arts and Sciences United, Catalogue of an exhibition at the Science Museum, London, published by Josiah Wedgwood & Sons Ltd, 1978

Kelly, Alison – *Decorative Wedgwood,* London, 1965

– *Wedgwood Ware,* London, 1970

Mankowitz, Wolf – *Wedgwood,* London, 1953

Meteyard, Eliza – *The Life of Josiah Wedgwood,* London, 1865-66

Meteyard, Eliza – *Wedgwood Trio by Meteyard* (reprint of three

earlier works – *Wedgwood and His Works,* 1873, *Memorials of Wedgwood,* 1874, and *Choice examples of Wedgwood's Art,* 1879), Pennsylvania, 1967

Minutes of the Wedgwood International Seminar, USA, 1965 et seq.

Proceedings of the Wedgwood Society, published by the Wedgwood Society, London, 1956 et seq.

Reilly, Robin – *Wedgwood,* London, 1989

Reilly, Robin and Savage, George – *Wedgwood, the Portrait Medallions,* London, 1973

Reilly, Robin and Savage, George – *The Dictionary of Wedgwood,* Woodbridge, 1980

Wedgwood Collectors Society Newsletter, P.O. Box 14013, Newark, NJ 07198

Wedgwood in London, Catalogue of the 225th Anniversary Exhibition, London, published by Josiah Wedgwood & Sons Ltd, 1984

Wedgwood Portraits and the American Revolution, Catalogue of an exhibition at the National Portrait Gallery, Smithsonian Institution, 1976

Wills, Geoffrey – *Wedgwood,* London, 1980, and New Jesey, 1989